I Am with You Always

**Other Loyola Press books
by Nicole Gausseron**

Believe That I Am Here
The Notebooks of Nicole Gausseron:
Book One

Walk with Me
The Notebooks of Nicole Gausseron:
Book Two

I Am with You Always

Always

The Notebooks
of Nicole Gausseron
BOOK THREE

Translated from the French by
William Skudlarek, O.S.B., and Hilary Thimmesh, O.S.B.

LOYOLAPRESS.

CHICAGO

LOYOLAPRESS.

3441 N. ASHLAND AVENUE
CHICAGO, ILLINOIS 60657
(800) 621-1008
WWW.LOYOLABOOKS.ORG

This book, published in three volumes, is a revised, reedited, and substantially expanded version of *The Little Notebook,* originally published as one volume in 1996 in the United States by HarperCollins.

Cover and interior design by Judine O'Shea
Cover photo: © Robert Everts/Getty Images

The ISBN for this volume is 0-8294-2039-8.

Library of Congress Cataloging-in-Publication Data
Gausseron, Nicole.
  Believe that I am here : the notebooks of Nicole Gausseron / translated from the French by William Skudlarek and Hilary Thimmesh.
      p. cm.
Rev. ed. of: The little notebook.
  ISBN 0-8294-1621-8
  1. Gausseron, Nicole—Diaries. 2. Catholics—France—Diaries. 3. Visions. 4. Jesus Christ—Apparitions and miracles—France—Chartres. 5. Compagnons du Partage. 6. Church work with the homeless—France—Chartres. 7. Chartres (France)—Church history—20th century. I. Gausseron, Nicole. Little notebook. II. Title.
  BX4705.G2636A3 2003
  282'.092—dc21
                                                    2003012152
Printed in the United States of America
04 05 06 07 08 09 10 M-V 10 9 8 7 6 5 4 3 2 1

Across the green fields of the Beauce, the rich wheat-growing region of France southwest of Paris, the famous silhouette of the cathedral of Notre-Dame de Chartres has beckoned to pilgrims for eight hundred years. Americans are likely to identify Chartres with the cathedral. To the people who live there, however, the city is not only the site of that great medieval structure but also a bustling regional center with typical modern economic and social problems, among them the needs of the poor.

Concern for the poor, particularly the homeless men who somehow survive on the fringes of society, led a woman of Chartres to help establish and to become the first director of a home for such men in 1981. She called it the Compagnons du Partage, a phrase not very satisfactorily translated as "Companions in Sharing." She started on a shoestring, aided by Bernard Dandrel—who would later found the first European food bank—and the first year in particular was touch and go.

The woman's name was Nicole Gausseron. She came from a distinguished family and was well educated. In fact she held a degree in British literature and taught for a time before her marriage to Philippe Gausseron. They both possessed that mix of intelligence and style that is characteristically French: understated, responsible, serious, but also attuned to warm friendship and the joy of living.

At the time that Nicole started her home for homeless men she was in her late thirties, and she and Philippe had three children—Laurette, Benoît, Thierry—ages seven to eleven. She had recently had the charismatic experience of baptism in the Holy Spirit, and she had come to know the poor through volunteer service with Secours Catholique, a national charitable organization of the French Catholic Church, of which Philippe was for ten years the local president.

Some of the poor, she discovered, needed not only a meal but a place to live and work, at least for a time. She set about providing such a place. The mayor of Chartres made an unused barracks on the edge of town available rent-free. Friends and well-wishers contributed odds and ends of furniture. The first day the doors were open, three men moved in; the second day, seven more. The Compagnons du Partage was off to a shaky start and depended on Nicole's constant attention to keep going.

The story of the Compagnons du Partage is more complicated than that, of course, but it is only partly the story of *The Notebooks of Nicole Gausseron,* which begins about four years after the founding of the Companions and transforms Nicole's experience into a universal and timeless story. Struggling to care for her two communities, as she calls them—her family and the men who came to live at the Companions—and always with inadequate resources, she was on the brink of abandoning her efforts after nine months of struggle when Pierre Maghin came to live with the Companions. Pierre was a priest of the Archdiocese of Paris who, with his bishop's blessing, had become a worker-priest in the late sixties. Bernard Dandrel had met him at a charismatic prayer meeting in Chartres and had approached him about becoming the director of the Community. On the day that he reserved the Sacrament in a makeshift chapel, Nicole knew the Compagnons du Partage would continue. It was for her the beginning of a new relationship with Jesus. In the celebration of the Eucharist in this modest setting, Jesus revealed his presence as a living person with feelings of his own, as a friend sharing her burdens and her joys, as the Lord speaking to her and to others through her about their indispensable part in his kingdom.

The Notebooks of Nicole Gausseron is a record of her encounters with Jesus, kept day by day in her *petit cahier,* her little notebook. The *Notebooks,* which are published in three volumes in this English edition, cover twelve years in Nicole's life, from the mid-1980s to the late 1990s. Book One, *Believe That I Am Here,* records the entries she made from March 22, 1985, to February 4, 1986. Book Two, *Walk with Me,* picks up where the first left off and takes us through the next five years, from February 5, 1986, to May/June 1991. The final volume, *I Am with You Always,* contains the entries she made between July 1992 and March 1997. The outward events of those years are lively, as the notebooks reveal—during that time Nicole raised a family while engaging in a demanding ministry to homeless men. We read of many joys—and a full measure of sorrow—in her life. But of even greater interest is the record Nicole kept of her inner life, especially the unfolding of her relationship with her friend Jesus.

A few words about how to read the *Notebooks* may be helpful. They are first of all virtually devoid of the reverential tone that we are accustomed to in works of piety. The style is much more like that of the Gospel accounts of Jesus' ministry—episodic, terse, objective. Continuity results from the development of central themes rather than sustained narrative. This method is incremental. It builds to something of great substance and consistency, but the reader can only know that—as Nicole came to know it—by starting with slight and fragmentary impressions.

Impressions is a key word. Nicole is not a visionary. In one of her first entries in the *Notebooks* she observes that the Lord is "seated beside us" but that "It's not a shadow or an apparition, but a presence." She often gives this presence a visual form and a location but never a detailed description.

The *Notebooks* present neither visions nor special revelations. Quite the contrary, Nicole earns a firm rebuff whenever she pushes the boundary of divine omniscience. "Is there a hell?" she asks, and Jesus replies, "Why are you so concerned about my Father's affairs?" She would like to know what will become of some unfortunate men, and Jesus tells her, "Do not try to know everything." This steadfast refusal to traffic in inside information about the spiritual realm, to claim privileged insights or private revelations, is to our minds one of the strongest arguments for the authenticity of these journals. The words of Jesus that Nicole reports tell us no more than the Gospels tell us.

The value of the *Notebooks* lies in their cogent reminder of how much the Gospels do tell us about Jesus and about ourselves in relation to him. There is nothing imaginary or remote about the Jesus who speaks to Nicole, smiles at her, is amused by her recollection of a refrain from an old love song, shows just a hint of weariness in reassuring her of his love for the umpteenth time, and once, to her astonishment, admits to a touch of jealousy. If the risk for believers is to relegate Jesus to resplendent glory as the *Kyrios,* the glorified Lord who is infinitely remote from daily life and correspondingly irrelevant, the Jesus who speaks in these pages insists on avoiding that risk by being one of us here and now. The bedrock reality is that he lives now and seeks a personal relationship with those who believe in him. This assurance is repeated and emphasized. "I am not an abstract idea or a system, but a living person." Nicole's repeated expression of concern for others occasions what is perhaps the most surprising theme in the *Notebooks,* one that may jar readers accustomed to easy pieties about serving God in one another. Jesus teaches Nicole that she must first of all respond directly to his love, attend to him, recognize his priority. She is free, as are all, to respond to him or not. He will not bind her; you don't bind those you love, and besides, he and his Father "have no need for puppets." But if she responds to his love, she must not forget him in her concern for others. In the end she can do nothing for others that he doesn't do through her, and he is also in those others, even the alcoholics who leave the Compagnons du Partage to all appearances no better off than when they came. Her responsibility and what she can do for others are limited; her relationship to Jesus is unlimited.

As Nicole continues to direct the Compagnons du Partage and to befriend the homeless and broken men who come to live and work together on the outskirts of Chartres, they, in turn, continue to reveal to her not only a Jesus who shares in the sufferings of this world but also a Jesus who loves her and all people with a love that is unconditional and unbounded.

One of the most important features of this remarkable journal is its implicit claim that a deeply personal and experiential knowledge of God goes hand in hand with deeply personal and experiential service to the poor. That claim is, of course, right at the heart of the New Testament: "How does God's love abide in anyone who has the world's goods and sees a brother or sister in need and yet refuses help?" (1 John 3:17). It is not uncommon, however, to find Christians—today as well as in times past—dividing themselves into opposing camps: those who claim to be true disciples of Jesus because they devote themselves to the spiritual life, and those who claim to be his true followers because they work for social justice. Nicole's experience of an intensely personal relationship with Jesus is grounded in her direct and loving contact with people who smell bad, who cheat, lie, and steal—even from her—and is thereby rendered all the more authentic.

Finally, a word should be said about the distinctly Catholic tone of this journal. Many, perhaps even most of, Nicole's dialogues with Jesus occur at Mass, usually in the Chapel of the Companions, where Pierre celebrates daily. Nicole often spends a half hour in prayer before the Blessed Sacrament.

Belief in the real presence of Jesus in the sacrament of the Eucharist and the act of remaining before it in an attitude of adoration provide Nicole with a way of focusing her attention and prayer. But it should also be noted that Nicole's practice of gazing at the consecrated communion wafer is more than just a method or technique for entering into a contemplative style of prayer. What it offers is a way of prolonging the act of praise and thanksgiving that is central to eucharistic worship and to the Christian life. Often she complains that it is hard to turn to praise in the midst of so much suffering. Patiently and lovingly, Jesus shows her that praise and thanksgiving are not ultimately to be located in feelings of well-being or in understanding why things are as they are but in maintaining a heart-to-heart relationship with him in spite of, and in the midst of, suffering.

Nicole's sense of the immediate presence of Jesus during the eucharistic celebration is rooted in and shaped by the Scriptures. On numerous occasions the dialogue between Nicole and Jesus is directly related to the scriptural passages that are read and meditated on in the celebration of the Eucharist. As one might guess from reading the *Notebooks,* the style of the celebration of the Eucharist in the Chapel of the Companions is quite different from the "oh-so-traditional" Sunday liturgies in her parish church. At the Community the pace is more relaxed, and there is ample opportunity for personal and spontaneous prayer. Nicole's words to Jesus are sometimes spoken aloud during these pauses for personal prayer, and on occasion Jesus asks her to convey his words to the small congregation that has come together for worship.

It may be helpful to note that the men who seek shelter at the Compagnons du Partage are welcomed in the name of Jesus but are not obliged to participate in any religious activities. The only conditions for living in the Community are that they not use drugs or alcohol and that they be willing to contribute to the work of the Community during their stay, which for most is a period of about three months. The work consists of collecting and repairing used goods and selling them in a secondhand store.

The Hermitage to which Nicole often refers is a farm about five miles from Chartres acquired in 1985 to provide more adequate living quarters for the Companions. The administrative center and place of work on the outskirts of the city is consistently referred to as the Community, and *Companion* is capitalized when it refers to a resident of the Compagnons du Partage.

In our judgment this remarkable journal modestly makes an extraordinary claim: that the Jesus of faith has given this teaching about himself to a woman of Chartres in our time. We have found that *The Notebooks of Nicole Gausseron* reveal their depths on repeated reading. When read straight through, the *Notebooks* give readers a sense of the movement of the journey that Jesus asks his followers to embark on, but each volume also rewards the random reader. On almost every page there is a word or statement that helps one understand more clearly and more concretely that a deep and personal relationship with Jesus—and, through Jesus, with God—is the heart and soul of the Christian life and that it contributes to the "weaving of the kingdom" when it is given expression in a preferential love for the poor.

William Skudlarek, O.S.B.
Hilary Thimmesh, O.S.B.

Saint John's Abbey, Collegeville, Minnesota

End of July

For the nth time I ask Jesus to come back and talk to me. For several months now I've been living what might be called a "normal" way of being a Christian. Like before? No. Now I am sure that Jesus is taking care of me and of the Community even more. Nothing has been easy since the Companions returned last September—quite the contrary. There is all sorts of stress, brawling, and a certain lethargy, perhaps, among the leadership, but I sense that I am powerfully and yet mysteriously helped. God the Father and his Son Jesus are moving from words to deeds, just as they promised, but the way they go about it baffles me. It's impossible to know in advance, or even to guess, when—in addition to how—they are going to help me. They did it, and they'll do it again. I'm not afraid.

In September we won't have anyone to be in charge of the Community, but we'll manage. I've just closed it down for the summer and sent all the Companions to the great outdoors.

It's time for vacation, for family, for silence. It was high time.

I've had a chance to rest this past week.

Sunday

I say to him:

> Do you see how good I've been? I'm accepting
> it, but I really would like you to return.

The reply comes after a bit of silence:

> ✝ *I have not gone away.*

Come back anyway.

> ✝ *I have told you everything. You have*
> *everything.*

All right.

It's useless to insist. I won't get anything more, and yet I
have a feeling—I know that this adventure is not over yet.

The little notebook has become public. It's not always easy
to receive or accept the reactions of one or another person.
On the whole I manage to stay calm, and I have made my
own the words that St. Bernadette said to her parish priest:
"My job is just to tell you, not to convince you."

Jesus is preparing me for something bigger. I don't have
any idea what it might be. The only thing I am sure of is
that it will be something big and beautiful. I'll leave it up
to him and follow with my eyes closed!

August 15

A concelebrated Mass. It's simple, peaceful, and devout—altogether perfect. The words addressed to Mary go right to my heart: they are so strong that there's no way that I can doubt them. Each word sounds as if it were spoken just to me. I feel a deep sense of serenity, in spite of the tears that are trickling down my cheeks. In all simplicity I accept being pampered, chosen, unique. Mary has become Nicole. It's crazy.

After Communion we speak to each other. I really want to tell him what's happening.

> Jesus, Jesus . . . I feel like I'm on the other
> shore. You've led me there and I've followed.
> I feel like a queen.

He smiles but does not answer.

A few moments later:

> It might seem as if I'm acting proud and being
> really stupid. I don't feel proud, though. Am I?
> Tell me.

> ☩ *No.*

A few moments later:

> I believe you Jesus. OK. I'm not proud. What is
> pride anyway? Tell me!
>
> ✝ *Pride, Nicole, is not preferring me.*

There you have it. I feel at the same time profoundly comforted and smothered by the simplicity of that answer.

October 8

After praying with three sisters and Pierre, we "snuggle" around the table of the Eucharist. As happens occasionally, this evening I sense that we are united as a family, and I sense that we have been given a gift.

We receive Communion together, and so, as the Eucharist is being distributed, we have to wait a bit with the host in our hands.

I am not so much speaking to him as to myself as I remark on how vulnerable the body of Christ is. Without anticipating any response I simply say to him:

> How vulnerable you are, Jesus. I could do just about anything with this little piece of bread.

Suddenly, a response I wasn't expecting springs up:

> ✝ *And you, too, are vulnerable.*

Then, a few moments later:

> That's right, Lord; I am. I can even be hurt by nothing at all. At times it's silly how vulnerable I can be. But why are you telling me this?

> ✝ *It is in the coming together of these two weaknesses that I create life.*

5

What do you mean?

✝ *Life, my life, springs up from this coming together.*

Joy floods my heart.

Then, a few days later, I am again involved in day-to-day affairs.

Let's go back a little.

We opened the Community on September 7, without anyone in charge, without a cook, and without anyone to answer the phone. During the first week Claude and I put in long days. (Claude is a volunteer, a retired business executive, whom Jesus sent to be my right-hand man.) We have to be all over the place, and at times I can't help smiling as I see Claude making the crust for a quiche or teaching a completely incapable Companion on KP how to make a chocolate mousse. All day long he was busy fixing things or helping unload the trucks. One doesn't get bored with the Companions. Actually, I make a pretty good chocolate mousse. Even my children say so, and that doesn't happen too often.

At the end of the second day, all Claude had to say was, "Thank goodness there are two of us."

We each have our job to do, like two riders on a tandem bicycle. The Companions notice it and feel the harmony in the Community. Claude has a good sense of which men are trustworthy, and so we put some of the Companions in charge of certain areas. In the evening and at night they are alone, and for a month now things have been running smoothly.

Now there's someone to answer the phone and to take charge of the kitchens. A certain rhythm has been restored and I feel relieved.

Yesterday there was a little incident, the kind that's happened before and will happen again. I had to rush out to the Community on Saturday morning because one of the Companions had overdosed and had to be hospitalized. He was hallucinating and didn't want to come out of his room.

As I am driving out to the farm, my heart is pounding and I feel that I simply don't have what it takes to handle a situation like this. I'm not afraid, but I am anxious.

> Jesus, don't you see? Anything can happen and
> I'm only a woman. All right. I'll do what I
> can, but it's not much. Help me. Please.

There wasn't much I could do for the Companion in the state he was in, but the EMTs whom I called used a lot of gentleness, patience, and humor and convinced him to go to the emergency ward.

Two days later the Companion came to collect his things and to apologize.

"Would you like a bite to eat?"

"No thanks. I don't deserve it. I'll be going. I'm very sorry."

So that's what I mean when I say I have the impression that I'm now involved in practical affairs. I gave Jesus my weakness and he made up for it.

March 16

The little notebook is off and running. Jesus is speaking to the heart of a number of readers, and at times, the letters they send are just amazing. Others are shocked, skeptical, even incensed that I would dance with Mary's son. Some, including those who are very close to me, think that I am conceited. *Who does she think she is? Shameless!*

I go about my business. I feel bad for them, not for me. If I irritate them, so be it! Why can't they understand what Jesus is saying? The living Jesus who once again is making himself known in order to enrich our faith. That little phrase of Bernadette to her parish priest keeps coming back to mind: "My job is just to tell you, not to convince you."

Once again, it's so simple. What's less simple for me is accepting the silence of Jesus.

Still, it's not the night. When I exasperate him with my requests to begin talking to me again, I always hear the same response:

✝ *I have already given it to you. I have already told you.*

I insist:

Come back; please come back to me!

The response is always the same:

> ✝ *You have everything. Now is the time for us to act. You know that very well.*

When I occasionally complain to Pierre, all he does is give me is a big smile and comment, "Just like the rest of us."

But I'm still not satisfied.

The weeks and the months go by, and I divide my life between the Companions during the week and my family in Paris on the weekends.

The days are full and demanding, but all in all, they're peaceful.

They said they were moving to deeds, and that's what they're doing. The Community of the Companions doesn't have a director, and yet it's moving along. The Companions themselves are taking charge of their own conduct. Claude and I do the best we can, and the help of the forty or so volunteers is both discreet and effective. I am often astounded at the peace that pervades this place, and I am not the only one.

We take the hard knocks as best we can. I am always saddened, and at times, devastated by the Companions' poverty and our inability to help them, but I am no longer overcome by a feeling of hopelessness. Twelve years of experience, and especially the little notebook, have taught me how to hand over to Jesus what I am unable to handle.

Jesus is taking care of the three men we just expelled. How? I don't know, but I am sure he is taking care of them, because we entrusted them to him. We couldn't do anything more for them. I am often surprised by what I say to Jesus:

> It's your turn, Jesus. I've done my part. I can't
> do anything more.

It also seems that Jesus is taking care of me in ways I couldn't imagine.

Jesus often said in the little notebook that he would make me a queen. Skeptic that I am, I said to him that I believed that would happen when I was dead, and he said to me:

> ✝ *I will make you a queen, the queen of my
> kingdom.*

I need to recognize that here, too, they are moving to deeds.

On one occasion Robert Masson invited me at the last minute to meet a man I had never heard speak and who had spent more than twenty years in a prison in Cuba. It had been a tough day with the Companions, and it took some doing to be able to slip away with some friends that evening to hear him talk about his experience. So I joined a small group of Christians who gathered to listen to a man by the name of Jorge Valls.

I still have the most glowing memory of that encounter. It is impossible, useless actually, to describe the outer and inner beauty of that man. You cannot forget a face like that: fire tempered by unspeakable sorrow. It's engraved in my memory. I was impressed, but not intimidated, by the intelligence and brilliance of some of the things he had to say, and I couldn't help noticing a profound weariness about him. He was stretched to the limit, almost without any strength left. Wanting to assuage the strain he was under and to give him a chance to take a little break, I stepped in to say a few words about what I meant by faith. I no sooner finished what I was saying than Valls remarked, "This woman is a mystic. She is a friend of God. Listen to her!"

Boom! Yes, boom. There's no other way to describe the shudder that went through my whole being.

Jorge spoke to us about suffering and especially about pardon. He pardoned his persecutors; I believe he has even gone so far as to love them. This man's holiness is beyond imagining.

Before I left, we spoke for a few moments, and I was confounded when I heard him thanking me. Now everything is backward.

Once again, I find myself in the hidden kingdom, in which unexpected shortcuts lead us to a brother. We are brother and sister because each of us, in our own way, has had an experience of the living Jesus. We have been cemented together by Jesus himself.

I had already experienced this same amazing and comforting encounter when I met Cardinal Gantin. Another person looks at you and sees you for who you are: unique, loved, and known in Jesus. What more can you ask for? Nothing.

In the car on the way back, I thank Jesus for having allowed me to meet such a witness, a true brother.

   ✝ *Queen, my little queen, I promised you!*

I shed silent tears of joy. Jesus knows what he is doing by comforting me for the many times in my youth that I thought I was nothing, no one.

Thank you.

There is no need to move up to praise; I am bathed in it. It's easy.

After the little notebook was published, a number of people confided in me, in us. Now there are more and more, and I'm a little afraid. I tell this to Jesus during the celebration of a Mass.

> Jesus, I'm afraid of becoming a celebrity. I don't want to distort anything. It's all in the little notebook. What I would like is for people to leave me alone and not put me on some stupid pedestal.

> ✝ *I have no such fear.*

Good. I can't keep from smiling. If he's not afraid, that means I should be able to just go on being myself.

> OK, Jesus. It's you first of all. With you in front of me, I'm not afraid.

The other day in a Mass at the Sisters of St. Paul, Pierre spoke about Jesus being wedded to our lives. I'm sure that's true, but I can't help thinking about all that's going on in Yugoslavia and elsewhere. How can you help but feel heartbroken?

I feel this so strongly that I can't refrain from criticizing him for the terrible state the world is in. It makes me sick.

Jesus, Jesus, those poor women in Yugoslavia, those camps in which innocent children are dying. How can a person reconcile those terrible scenes with the love that you are pouring out over us, over me, at this very moment?

It's a cry of rebellion within me.

> ✝ *I did not ask you to carry this world. I am the one who carries it.*

I can't accept that.

> Too easy, Jesus. They're dying. Can't you see?

> ✝ *You do not understand.*

Then explain what you mean!

> ✝ *Do not carry the world. I did not ask you to carry it.*

Then what am I to do? They're dying, and I can't stand it.

> ✝ *Pray.*

Jesus, Jesus. They're being raped, killed. Families are torn apart. You want me not to mind?

> ✝ *No.*

It's a wrestling match. I refuse to put up with an intolerable situation and to be content with just praying. I manage to quiet down, though, and a bit of peace returns. I look at the bread that has become the body of Christ.

Your body, Jesus?

✝ *Yes.*

Suddenly, mysteriously, it seems that everything becomes clear.

Jesus, Jesus, are you jealous?

✝ *Yes.*

And what you want is that, at this moment, I belong totally to you?

✝ *Yes.*

To no one else?

✝ *No one.*

I manage to say:

Here I am.

But a few seconds later I can't help asking him:

And the world?

✝ *It is I who will look after it, not you. When you are with me, give me your undivided attention.*

And you will take care of it?

✝ *I will take care of it.*

Amen.

There have been other occasions when I have realized how attentive Jesus has been to me only after the fact. There are often occasions when, without saying anything to anyone about it, I secretly wish that a solution might be found for some difficulty or that something will turn out differently. They are like passing thoughts, and I don't hang on to them, because they are things that don't depend on me.

Jesus promised that he would surprise me.

Without any effort on my part, although I did hope it would happen, some people from Chartres have become true friends, thanks to the Companions.

During my brief stays at Saint-Benoît, I sometimes suffered a little bit because I really didn't feel like part of the community. They were all in the sanctuary of the basilica concelebrating the Mass, while I, out in the nave, felt more like a spectator.

That's just normal, though. I accepted the way it was, without hoping or expecting that things would change. They're monks; they live in community. I'm married and have a family. My community is elsewhere. That's the way it is. But then, without willing it and without doing anything to bring it about, it happened that a bond was established between me and some of the monks, and I began to feel a little more at home. I was still surprised. Jesus knows how hopelessly sentimental I am and he looks after me.

Jesus knows each of us intimately and gives us all the gifts we need. I, and many other people I know, can give numerous examples of this.

I was in my car one day thinking about this when I heard Jesus say to me:

✝ *The secret of the king.*

I didn't have time to talk about this with him because Pierre, Bernard, and I had to meet a young woman in the chapel and pray with her. We would come back to it later.

In the oratory of Saint-Benoît-sur-Loire, I finally have time to be with him, and I ask him:

The secret of the king, Jesus?

And since I'm feeling it, I can't refrain from adding:

Have you come back to talk to me, Jesus?

I feel completely calm and at peace.

✝ *Yes, I still have some things to teach you.*

It's Lent, but so what: Alleluia!

Tell me the secret. Why is it secret? I have the impression that this is something important for you.

✝ *You. Me. The others do not need to know.*

I make myself become silent, and I think of the Song of Songs, of the beloved. I always found that passage very moving, but I always thought it applied only to certain chosen souls, and I certainly wasn't one of those. It is such a powerful passage, almost too powerful. It was practically indecent.

Jesus, are you the beloved?

✝ *Yes.*

And one should keep silent?

✝ *Yes.*

I weep quietly. Here it is in the middle of Lent, and he has come back (that's not really true; I know he never left) to speak to me of the secret. I am happy, peacefully and profoundly happy, perfectly relaxed.

Jesus, it's impossible to put this experience into words.

✝ *There is no need. Words are useless.*

Why is that?

✝ *Because this secret is not spoken or written. It bursts into daylight without words.*

Do you mean to say that this moment we are living is somehow going to burst into daylight?

✝ *Yes.*

How?

✝ *You will see.*

Give me a hint.

✝ *When you speak about me, with me, it will burst forth. When you are silent, or looking at somebody, it will burst forth, too.*

It's up to you?

✝ *Yes, it is up to me.*

That's why I need not fear?

✝ *Yes. If I am with you, what can possibly happen to you?*

Jesus loves us. Jesus is the Lover!

March

Pierre speaks about our Father in heaven, whom he calls "Papa." It's impossible for me to call him that, and I tell Jesus so.

We have to make up or find another name.

No reply.

You are a lot more than my father?

Even if he doesn't know it, I admire my father and love him dearly. Whenever I am with the Companions, I often have the impression that I am walking in his footsteps. My father taught me so much.

✝ *Yes.*

Which is to say?

✝ *My Father is your breathing; he is the breath of the world.*

End of March

Our dialogue seems to be starting up again. It makes me happy to know that the Lord wants me to depend on him unconditionally. Total confidence, nothing more, nothing less.

That's not too difficult for me right now because I am letting go completely. He knows better than I do what is to be done, so let him do it! It's simple and relaxing, because he's the one who is doing the work.

I have a little time today because the Companions are behaving, and Pierre went in my place to see a former Companion who is in a psychiatric hospital.

We speak to each other as I walk along a sun-drenched street:

> Jesus, do you still have some things to teach me?
>
> ✝ *Yes.*
>
> Can you speak to me about eternity with you?
>
> ✝ *That is not something you can learn about.*
>
> Then what?
>
> ✝ *You are living it already.*

Do you mean to say that your eternity begins here below? I can understand that. But what about death? I still think it's a scandal, an amputation. Whatever one thinks about it, it's a separation.

✝ *Yes.*

I know that he'll explain it to me later. There are times when I feel so happy to be alive—quite often, actually. Even now when I feel run down because of a toothache or frazzled by too many little things to take care of, I still love life and the feeling of being alive. To be able to feel this way is a real blessing. I don't want to die, and I would like to believe, not just with my head but with my whole being, that happiness awaits us after our death.

Later that evening

It's peaceful and prayerful, and as I listen to Pierre's homily, I meditate on his reference to Jesus as "one with us" and Son of God at the same time.

Thanks to the little notebook, to this awesome exchange I have with you, I am, at least to some degree, "at home with you," Jesus.

✝ *Much more than that.*

What do you mean?

✝ *You are mine.*

Once again, I begin to tremble, trying to hide my tears as best I can. The force of his words is beyond belief.

Yours?

✝ *Yes.*

For the first time, I can say to him in all sincerity:

I feel so unworthy.

✝ *In your own eyes, yes, but not in mine.*

Voilà. Breathtaking, and yet so simple.

22

So that is the meaning of your eternity, Jesus?

✝ *A bit of my eternity.*

The next day

A little more about your eternity, Lord. I would like to enter it just as I am right now, without any fear, sure that I will be even happier than I am now.

I say this inside of myself, not really sure of what I am saying. Jesus is silent.

I enter more deeply into this silence. (I was going to say, into my soul.)

✠ *Do not be afraid, Nicole. Do not be afraid.*

Please say more.

✠ *My eternity is being in me. Do you understand?*

Yes, I think so. What you mean is that in some way I will be in your arms, in your love?

✠ *Nicole, I am alive.*

I remember how, about twenty years ago, I consoled a little girl in my catechism class who had lost her brother. All the pupils in the class, including my two sons, were in tears, and the only thing I could say to her was, "He's in the arms of Jesus."

April 5

I hear the text from Isaiah 49:1–6 as meant for me. I am favored, protected, chosen.

Pierre insists that Jesus was obedient to the end, that he consented.

> Jesus, you consented right from the start. You are both God and man. As for me, I did not ask for anything.

> ✝ *And that is why it is necessary that I walk before you.*

> You show the way?

> ✝ *Yes.*

A little later:

> ✝ *I am* alive: *I am the Son of God. I am not a concept. If your faith in me is to be true and sure, while you are alive you have to keep on moving closer to my death. Do you understand?*

> Yes, I think so.

It's a strange Lent for me this year. There are moments when my heart leaps for joy. I enjoy a feeling of peace and let myself be bathed by the words *mine* and *in me*. I don't try to figure them out or to intellectualize them. I keep them within myself.

It's so easy and simple. I experience such peace that I'm afraid that one of these days I'm going to be hit on the head by a falling brick!

April 24

Here we are in Corsica with the Sisters of Bethlehem. When I wasn't able to make a retreat in Assekrem, this beautiful and hidden spot was offered to me. Beauty, sun, and solitude guaranteed! I am in charge of the three Companions who are working here, and I take my meals with them. In the late afternoon I go to Vespers and Mass with the three sisters. Since I have a lot of time and can keep my mind uncluttered, maybe we will be able to have some good conversations. Maybe!

Before I left, as I was thanking him for all that he was doing for the Companions, Jesus said to me:

> ✢ *I already told you: You will do greater things than I.*

The words are so astounding that I hardly have the courage to write them down.

A little later I say:

> Tell me what you mean!

> ✢ *We are two. You do your work, and you let me do mine.*

I have such a hard time accepting these words, and once again, I am so afraid that I am making them up that I decide right there and then to go to the sisters' little chapel.

It's me, Jesus. Now you listen to me. I am ready to tear up this page that I've just written. How can you possibly want me to do more than you? You healed people, saved them, multiplied the loaves. . . .

✝ *But it is I who will do these things with you. It is I who will do them!*

But I still feel doubtful and somewhat uneasy.

✝ *You are afraid, Nicole.*

Yes, it's true. I am afraid. It's too much for me. But then I am suddenly reassured, comforted.

Yes, Jesus, I am afraid.

✝ *Do not be afraid, Nicole. It is I who will do all this.*

April 25

The next day at Mass, I try to descend to the depths of my inner being and to hear what Jesus may want to say to me. The singing of the sisters, a cross between Byzantine and Gregorian styles, is comforting, and I think I understand, or rather, that I "make my own" what Jesus wanted to tell me yesterday.

> What you want is that I be your instrument of glory?
>
> ✝ *Yes.*
>
> I'll be sprinkled with it, but the glory is you, the Glorious One.
>
> ✝ *Yes.*

I have the impression that he is smiling, and I finally feel peaceful. I needed five days here to feel that peace, and if I don't feel it, I get anxious.

> We make everything so complicated, Jesus. But it's really so very simple.
>
> ✝ *Have no fear. Do not be afraid. We are moving on to deeds, just as we promised you.*

It takes time, Jesus, to really integrate everything that you teach me, for it to go beyond my
mind and my feelings down to the very depths
of my being. Do you understand what I mean?

✝ *Yes, Nicole, and I allow for the time you need.*

April 26

Jesus says to me as I am walking to the chapel:

> ✠ *All time is mine.*

Do you mean to say that eternity is yours, Jesus?

> ✠ *No. All time is mine. I devote all my time to
> you, to all people, on this earth.*

Why do you tell me once again how infinitely
patient you are, Jesus?

> ✠ *In order to reassure you. Do not be afraid.
> Stay calm and peaceful: what you are not
> able to do, I will do with you tomorrow.*

I think about these words and meditate on them during
Mass, but I become terribly upset.

Ever since I've arrived there's a little voice inside my head
that I try to resist but that keeps on reminding me of all the
people who don't like me and who have done things to
upset me. I'm furious because I don't want to be weighed
down by such thoughts, but I don't seem to be able to con-
trol them.

I thought I had finally gotten rid of them, and then, right at
the beginning of the Mass, I start thinking about someone

who is close to me but who has been snubbing me for a long time. These thoughts are so unnerving that I can't concentrate. It's ridiculous and yet unbearable. Since I'm unable to stop feeling like a wretched little accountant, I simply say to Jesus:

What's going on, Jesus? Why am I letting myself be filled with these thoughts and images? It's all true, but it seems so petty. Help me!

✞ *Do what I do, Nicole.*

What you do?

✞ *Do not linger with them. Keep moving, as I do.*

Jesus, I didn't do anything to harm them. Why don't they like me? I didn't do anything to them.

✞ *Keep moving, Nicole.*

Jesus, listen to me! You moved along, all right, but I am sure you felt sad.

✞ *Yes.*

That's what I mean.

✞ *Keep moving, Nicole. Look at all the others that I have given you.*

In the silence that follows I feel better. Jesus doesn't make fun of my feelings. He takes them into account and looks on me with love. It's true. There's a long list of people whom I just happened to meet and who subsequently became my allies and even my "accomplices."

After Mass, a half hour of adoration. I make my thanksgiving and hear Jesus say to me:

✝ *I believe in you, Nicole.*

Boom!

I weep quietly. After a few minutes I am able to say:

We usually put it just the other way around.

Then a little later:

You know, you really take a lot of risks, Jesus.

✝ *No more than Philippe and the children. They also believe in you.*

A moment of silence.

Jesus, you are completely overwhelming. In no time at all, you have changed my confusion into a joy so strong I can hardly bear it. You don't seem to believe in letting me just relax.

✝ *I have already told you, Nicole, that I am not offering you an easy and quick way to travel.*

Amen. Rather, Alleluia, as Pierre and the sisters would say.

From time to time, the face of Jesus appears on the host. I don't ask any questions. It's there but not very clearly.

Monday, June 7, and Tuesday, June 8

Alone in the chapel of the Companions, I tell him once again how grateful I am for all he does in the Community. Everything is running smoothly, and I have never felt so light, despite the weight of these men and their suffering.

As I look at the host and offer my prayers of thanksgiving, I feel content. Then the appearance of the host begins to change: surrounded by a heavy golden wreath, it moves toward me and then retreats. I close my eyes. I am very calm, and so this can't be the result of my imagination. I open my eyes and see the same thing happening again. So be it.

Jesus, you are living.

Perhaps he will explain this to me tomorrow.

I take my leave.

Tuesday

Do you have something to tell me, Jesus?

✠ *I encircle you, enfold you with my tenderness.*
Let go.

At the celebration of the Eucharist, we read from the Gospel according to Matthew 5:13–16: "You are the light of the world."

June 9

The second letter of St. Paul the Apostle to the Corinthians (3:11): "For if what was set aside came through glory, much more has the permanent come in glory!"

That heavy wreath of gold, Jesus, is it your glory?

✝ *Yes.*

Thank you, Jesus.

A week off with Philippe and a friend in the sun, the calm, and the magnificent aromas of this little corner of heaven. I can forget about everyone (except the children, of course) and regain my strength.

Jean-Claude, one of the dependable Companions, told me as I was leaving: "Do not worry. You won't even have to give us a call. Everything will be fine."

And I don't call.

On two occasions I visit Jesus in the lovely church of Moustiers. It's empty and we have a chance to talk to each other.

✝ *I will take you on a long journey, Nicole.*

Very well.

Then on the second visit two days later:

I don't know where you are going to lead me,
and I'm not at all worried. You can do anything,
and so I'm not going to ask you where.

It's curious, this absence of curiosity on my part. That's what I'm thinking as I look at Jesus on the cross. A little bit of progress, perhaps?

Jesus, you're not too disappointed with me?

✣ *No. You let me fill up your lamp. Keep on.*

He smiles and I leave the chapel happy. The happiness comes from him.

End of July

We're closing down the Community for more than a month. I will have more time for him. Jesus has certainly not been very talkative, but I'm not troubled; I know he's not far away.

As I'm walking to church to go to Mass in a little village of the Cévennes, I try to get our conversation started again. I now have some time to ask him what he means by this "long journey."

> You will take me on a long journey, Jesus. No use in asking you where. You don't answer.

> ✝ *No, you will not receive an answer. I am going to surprise you.*

I think about the road he led me down during these past ten years.

> You came to me to tell me that you are living. And it's a year now that you've shown me that you're moving on to deeds. Is that what this is all about, Jesus?

> ✝ *Yes.*

And now?

> ✝ *Together we are going to go farther.*

August

The bishop celebrates the Mass and the cathedral is full.

I feel like Mary (. . . ? . . !), loved, chosen, called on. My serenity shows it.

With a peaceful heart I tell him once again:

> I am your servant, Jesus. I will follow you.

A few seconds later he speaks to me:

> ✝ *Dispossess yourself even more, Nicole.*

I confess that I'm a little taken aback. I tell him so.

> But I've done that; I'm doing it. You know that I abide by what you say. What else do you want of me?

> ✝ *Dispossess yourself even more, Nicole.*

> Dispossess myself of what?

I wait for a reply. I really am letting go. What is it that I am still hanging on to? I have absolutely no idea.

> Tell me, Jesus.

> ✝ *Of your fears, of your sufferings, those that have been entrusted to you.*

I mull this over a little; it's true that I am affected by the anguish and fear that I perceive in others.

> But I can't do otherwise, Jesus. That's what compassion is all about.

> ✝ *Give your load to me. You are only a link in the chain. I am the one who bears the weight.*

Silence. I think I understand.

Mid-August 1993

I went up to the farm two times just so the few Companions who are there wouldn't feel too abandoned. I also spent some time with Jesus.

During my time of adoration, first I see the figure of Jesus, and then several faces pass before me. An old woman, a younger woman, and then Jesus again.

Strange! I feel at peace, but I don't understand what he wants to say to me.

Could this be my imagination, Jesus?

It's while reading the Gospel of the day, as I'm accustomed to do at the end of each period of adoration, that I have the impression that he is replying to my question.

Matthew 19:13–15.

September

The Community is doing fine. The Companions themselves are in charge. There are ups and downs, of course,
but even with twenty Companions, things are fine.

I'm managing to keep faithful to a period of adoration
when Pierre is not there to celebrate Mass in our little
chapel. I have the time to visit with the Lord and his Father
since I am there all alone with them.

On several occasions, I see faces on the exposed host:
young people, old people, and then Jesus himself.

> Are these the faces of people you are sending to
> me, Jesus?
>
> ✝ *Yes.*
>
> Do you want me to tell them about you and how
> I depend on you?
>
> ✝ *Yes.*

Just a few hours later, an older woman and then a younger
one who needed comforting sought me out. Over the
course of the next few days, a telephone call here, a meeting there, confirmed what I saw in the host.

I would like to tell Jesus that he shouldn't send me too much; I'm afraid of becoming overloaded! But they know what they're doing. They're perfectly capable of giving me a little respite, as they've always done in the past.

Mid-September

A strange impression of being nowhere. A conviction that it's Jesus who is making this community work. I'm there, right in the middle of them, quite a bit of the time, actually, but it's not I who am responsible for the peace that is there. He is. They are. When I go from an office to the kitchen, and then from the sales room to a storage room or to one of the outbuildings, I feel like I am being accompanied by a very strong presence. Sure, I drop a word here and there, tell this one to shape up, make sure that someone cleans up the restrooms (and how!), answer the telephone, and so on. I'm not schizophrenic, but deep down I know that I am being "indwelled." It's not pride; it's just a fact.

Up until now, I had never understood what Paul meant when he said, "It is not I who act, but God who acts in me." At the same time, Paul is anything but laid-back; he fights, writes, even "flies off the handle." But now I think I understand—not with my head, but with my whole being—what Paul means. I know, I know. . . . Who am I to compare myself with Paul? But the dynamics are the same.

Now and then I talk to the Lord about this impression I have of being "nowhere." He is there to listen to me, whatever state of mind I'm in, but I am still somewhat hesitant to tell him about this impression I have. One night, in the chapel, I have the courage to say to him, albeit timidly:

> Jesus, you have spoiled me. Thanks to you I am happy. But, Jesus, why this impression of being nowhere? Do you understand what I am talking about?

> ✝ *Yes.*

Tears of joy. He doesn't rebuke me at all.

> Could you explain? That would really help.

> ✝ *Nicole, we have now begun to act, and you are letting us.*

> I'm still not sure I understand.

> ✝ *You are with them, with the world, but at the same time you are ours.*

> I am tied to you in some way?

> ✝ *Yes, but you do not know where we are going to send you; you do not know our plans for you and with you.*

> And so I have this feeling of being nowhere. I understand, Jesus.

I have to let go. Without a doubt, we always keep coming back to these same words.

Jesus smiles and my confidence is restored.

October 13

Pierre, two sisters of St. Gervais, and a brother. We pray before the Blessed Sacrament. Once again, faces pass before me. I am not disturbed. I close my eyes and open them again to be sure my imagination is not playing tricks on me.

A few seconds later another host surrounded with gold detaches itself from the first.

Lord? The second host?

✝ *That is you, each one of you. Let me be your inner sparkle. Only that.*

The intensity of what I saw stays with me over the following days.

October 17

St. Paul speaks to us of "absolute certainty." That's too strong for me, and I can't help thinking that Paul is being a little "puffed up" to speak like this. Those are two strong words: *absolute certainty.*

The next morning

As I jumped out of bed to attack a new day with my usual "Up and at 'em, Jesus, the two of us," the response of Jesus came to me. That morning I wasn't feeling very upbeat when I said "the two of us." The previous evening I had listened to a story of terrible suffering, and I was still feeling very downcast this morning.

> ✝ *I have lifted everything up on my cross, Nicole. That is what is certain.*

On your cross, Jesus?

> ✝ *Yes.*

I was instantly blinded by this truth.

> I understand, Jesus. All the evils we do, the dishonest acts and deeds we commit or imagine, they're all taken up by you on your cross, all of them.

> ✝ *Yes.*

> The twisted, the perverse, the impure.

> ✝ *Yes.*

> Jesus, Jesus, how you suffered!

I weep, and all I can do is repeat *Jesus.*

Were you disgusted, Jesus?

✝ *No, Nicole.*

Crushed?

✝ *Yes, it was heavy.*

Silence. I am, as it were, at the foot of the cross.

A little later:

Jesus, is it even heavier today because people continue to sin?

✝ *No.*

Why not?

✝ *Because every time you draw from my cross, you bring me joy.*

So your death was not in vain?

✝ *No, it was not.*

October 19–21

A friend invited me to come to speak about the poor to a gathering of priests. There were almost six hundred priests assembled in the basilica. It was all the more impressive because everything was so unpretentious and yet so well organized.

My meeting with the priests about the poor was very moving. They listened eagerly to what I had to say and were even deferential. Yet, deep down, I felt sad. Is it because I sense that most of them are tired, worn out, actually? During the meal that I share with them, I sense a deep loneliness in them.

All alone in the basilica, I retire to a little corner to pray. It's my desert day while they are on an outing to Ars. I tell Jesus about my sorrow.

> We are the richest people in the world, Lord, but you'd never guess it. Where is the joy, Lord?

He does not answer right away.

> Where's the certitude that you revealed to me?

Silence.

> Jesus, what does one have to do to achieve it?

✝ *A double simplicity.*

What do you mean?

✝ *The simplicity of being what you are,*
accepting who you are.

And the other, Jesus?

✝ *The simplicity of accepting the immensity of*
my love.

I understand, and at that very moment the face of the stone statue of Mary I am looking at seems to come to life; the features become indistinct and blurry, and then it's Jesus who is looking at me with infinite love, and then again, it's Mary. I am bathed in overwhelming tenderness.

It's crazy. They are alive, both of them. They are real. They go ahead of us, accompany us, carry us.

It's crazy, but it's terribly true.

February

A full day at the Companions—nothing really important to deal with, but all sorts of little things to take care of with this one or that. I listen to a Companion who returned from a construction job at the Sisters of Bethlehem. He tells me with an air of seriousness about the peace that he found there and of his great respect for the sisters.

"They're shut up," he tells me, "but it's not like me."

. . . ! . . . ? "What do you mean, Jacques?"

"They chose that way of life. But when I was in prison, it was because they put me there. I know what their life is like, and I really respect them."

This wild man who has spent quite a bit of time in prison, who's not at all community-minded, is now telling me that he has found a second family. I know I'm being naive, but I can't help saying, "But you've put all that behind you now."

"No," he replies. "Even if you don't want to, you can always start drinking again. But now I have some guardrails; that's what you are for me. And I really feel at peace when I'm working for the sisters all by myself."

A little later, another Companion says to me with childlike amazement, "I don't have the least desire to do anything stupid for the time being. I'm really fine here." And then he adds, "I hope it keeps up."

This is something to be happy about and give thanks. That's what I do as I am giving a tour to some friends from Orléans who have come to visit the Community. And then I hear Jesus saying to me:

✝ *I told you.*

You told me what?

✝ *You will do greater things than I.*

I'm a little astounded, but even more overcome by doubt. There's so much to do that I don't have the time to continue the discussion during the afternoon. We'll take it up again this evening at the Eucharist.

Evening

I speak to him:

> Jesus, what I just heard was overwhelming. How
> could I possibly do more than you? I haven't
> cured the sick or performed miracles as you did.

A little later:

> Explain it, Jesus. I don't want to become
> paranoid.

> ✝ *When I performed miracles, it was my Father
> and I. Do you understand?*

Yes.

> ✝ *And today you have added your part.*

That's the "greater" you spoke about?

> ✝ *Yes. Without you, without all of you, we would
> not have been able to give this joy to the
> Companion. Greater because you added your
> contribution. Do you understand?*

I think I do. I let these words penetrate my being, and I
simply keep repeating that Jesus needs us. It's true that
three—I should really say four; we mustn't forget the Holy

Spirit—can do more than two. But better? Greater? That continues to bother me.

The next day. I'm slow to understand, but since I know that Jesus is perfectly aware of this condition, I don't pester him. I'm sure that I will be enlightened.

February 13

It was time for things to slow down; I was at the end of my rope. In the little chapel at Mieussy, empty but welcoming, I am finally relieved of my fatigue and worries, and I am able to say to him:

> Greater. That still rubs me the wrong way. This contribution I made didn't produce anything "greater."

> ✝ *You are wrong.*

> What do you mean?

> ✝ *Nicole, you are distorting my words. I am God. Do not compare yourself with me. Work with me.*

> Explain what you mean.

> ✝ *Your way of understanding* greater *is that you are going to do my work, in my place, like me. That is impossible!*

> Yes . . . ?

✝ *With your human contribution, you will*
  prolong my activity. That is the reason what
  you do will be greater. Do you understand?

Yes, I think so. You are the one who will be the
"doer," and I, we, we are and will be nothing but
"unlockers." Is that more or less it?

✝ *Yes.*

I begin to reconsider an idea that so often vexes me. Why
were there so few miracles, so few cures in the time of
Jesus? Why this reluctance? It's as if one had to force Jesus
to do something he really would rather not do. And still . . .

✝ *You already have the answer, Nicole.*

Did you already tell me?

✝ *Yes.*

The marvelous deed isn't the miracle. Is that it,
Jesus? It's sending someone back to your Father,
right?

✝ *Yes.*

And we who contribute to your kingdom with
the help of the Holy Spirit, we send people back
to you?

✝ *Yes.*

To come right down to it, everyone has his or her own job
to do. The miraculous, the impossible, that's your part. To

try (and that's the right word) to love others unconditionally, that's what Jesus asks of us.

> You want us to make a contribution, but you
> definitely do not want us to take your place,
> Jesus. You want us to make a decision for you,
> desire you?

> ✝ *Yes.*

I think he smiles.

I've finally understood. It's really quite simple.

February 19

I meditate on the answers of Jesus, and despite the peace
that is within me, I still want to make his words clearer.

Pierre had given me John 14:9–14 to meditate on: "I will
do whatever you ask in my name."

> I know that I've already asked you this, Jesus,
> but I'll do it again. What do you mean by "in
> my name"? You do not grant all we ask of you;
> that's for sure. And I accept it. But "in your
> name"?

> ✝ *That which you ask for in faith. Now do you*
> *understand better?*

> Yes, I think so.

I reflect on this for a moment and then say to him:

> Yes, I think I understand. When I ask you
> something like a child without any hidden
> agenda (this part is really important), you will
> do it?

> ✝ *Yes.*

> It's not me, but you who will do it?

✝ *It is your faith that will enable me to do it.*

So one comes back to the relationship, Jesus. "In my name": does that mean that the two of us are bound together, and there is no hidden agenda on my part other than trust?

✝ *Yes.*

Therefore, it's not just because of my exertion, the amount of time I spend praying, or how difficult it will be for me to ask you something. Do I have it right?

✝ *Yes. It is through your availability to others and your trust in me that I will do it.*

I understand.

So there's no reason for me to be so adamant. All we have to do is be faithful.

Your way of responding will not always be obvious. It can be . . . mysterious?

✝ *Of course. A relationship involves the mystery of the other. You know that very well.*

End of February

The Gospel is Matthew 7:7–12: "How much more will your Father in heaven give good things to those who ask him?"

> You're saying that you only give good things, Jesus. I'm not so sure. What I am sure of is that you are concerned for us. But how can one accept, how can one understand suffering, wickedness, the hopelessness of certain people, and . . . but that's enough.

This text has always baffled me.

> ☩ *You are forgetting my dimension, Nicole: eternity.*

For me, eternity continues to be the Great Unknown.

> ☩ *No. Eternity is me.*

I allow these words to sink deeply into me.

What it comes down to is that we mustn't allow ourselves to be overcome by what we don't understand, not even by what is unsupportable, but only by Jesus himself.

Third week of Lent

I always feel sorrowful during this time when Jesus is on his way to Calvary. Son of God and yet fully man. As I am listening to the Gospel from John 11:45–57, I cannot help saying to him:

> How terribly you suffered, Lord. You, the Son of God! Did you know ahead of time what was in store for you?

> ✝ *No.*

I allow the silence to descend over me.

Jesus speaks again:

> ✝ *It's something like with you.*

What do you mean?

> ✝ *It is in the relationship with me that you move forward, that you make decisions, that you accept what I give you to live out.*

But only a little, Jesus. The two of you are one.

✝ *Yes. But like you, I did not follow a program.*
I lived every moment in relation with my
Father. Do you understand?

Yes, I think I am getting it, at least a little. At the end of the
Eucharist it appears that he is saying to everybody:

✝ *Do not make plans; above all, do not make a*
program.

Wednesday of Holy Week

This large building is empty of seminarians. There are only a few around the place. A priest friend of mine and some of the others on the staff concelebrate in a simple and bare chapel.

The Lord is present and those who have been invited are in communion. I know that Jesus is going to speak to me.

The Gospel of Matthew 26:14–25: "The one who has dipped his hand into the bowl with me will betray me."

Why do you share this morsel with Judas, Jesus?

✝ *I am with him to the end, even in the evil he does.*

These words knock me over. A human with humans, a human gesture of sharing and God, the Son of God who is present with us.

What about me, Jesus? And the rest of us. What are we to do? The same thing? Is that what you're trying to say?

✝ *No.*

Then please explain.

✝ *Stop before you get there. Do not lower yourself. Let me bear the evil that you will encounter. Me. That is what I will do on the cross after Holy Thursday.*

Later:

✝ *Do not be upset. I will bear it.*

The host is raised. A shadow passes over it, and for a few seconds a barely distinguishable face is drawn. The Lord glances at me and seems to be saying to me:

✝ *Do not be upset. I am here.*

I am bowled over but at peace.

June _____

I began thinking about death as I was walking slowly and in silence. My thoughts about death were always the same. If only we were absolutely sure that death is a new birth, life in abundance. Pascal's wager is not enough; we need this certitude.

> Jesus, I have the impression that some people are like insects flying into a windowpane. They want to see what's behind it, but the glass is in the way.

> ✞ *Get rid of the glass. You have created it, not I.*

There is no glass.

End of June, July, beginning of August

These past weeks I've been feeling very heavy, or rather empty. It's as if I were totally drained. I know that the end of the school year is always a busy time, that it was difficult to close down the community for summer vacation, and that the continual betrayal of trust on the part of the Companions and even of some of the volunteers gets me down. But what's going on with me? I've had to deal with these sorts of things before—with much worse things, in fact.

I feel heavy and sad, and that élan that draws me out of myself even when I don't feel like it seems somewhat damaged. I hate to fake it, to play a role, or to pretend to be happy when, in fact, I'm feeling down.

No faking it, no silly heroics. I feel incredibly vulnerable and am often on the verge of tears over nothing. A trifle upsets me, and sometimes I am awakened in the middle of the night by a dull anguish whose origin I cannot pinpoint.

What is happening to me?

My usual response to this kind of torment is to find some silent time and get to work on some inner housekeeping. I try to do this as honestly as I can and with as much of a sense of humor as I can muster.

But all for naught; since I can't do any better, I try to accept my condition and give myself some TLC. It's the best I can do. What it comes down to is gently saying to myself, "Nicole, let Nicole be without peppering her with all these questions that don't have an answer." I accept the present, life as it is, and I indulge myself with some little trifles.

But the heaviness is always there, and Philippe asks me, "What's the matter? Are you having trouble with depression?"

No, I'm sure it's not that, and yet . . .

August 8

It was only yesterday that everything seemed to become clear. I was away for two weeks on vacation, roughing it but still managing to get a lot of rest. When I got back home, everything was so quiet, and I simply burst into tears all alone in my living room.

> I've had it, Jesus; I've had it. I know it's because you don't talk to me anymore like you used to.

How am I supposed to resign myself to this absence when once there was Jesus, and even his Father?

"Like the rest of us," Pierre tells me.

But this absence—you have to have known the presence to understand this void, this pain. I've no right to complain, because I've received so much. But this absence.

> Do something, both of you. I've had it.

I sobbed for quite a while.

> If my problem is depression, I'm willing to go into treatment. If it's not that, tell me what it is.

That was the gist of my prayer.

I give them some time to reply, and I decide that I'll just take my time before leaving the house to go to the chapel of the Companions at the Hermitage.

On the way there I very gently ask them:

> I'm experiencing the dark night of the soul? Is that it?
>
> ✝ *No.*
>
> What then?
>
> ✝ *It is the shadow.*
>
> What shadow?
>
> ✝ *You are in our shadow, the shadow of our love. Do you understand?*
>
> Yes.

A harsh and irresistible peace comes over me. All is calm and I have a profound sense that I have received the response I was asking for.

A few minutes later:

> Why a shadow? Why? Are you continuing to mold and shape me?
>
> ✝ *Yes.*
>
> Tell me why.
>
> ✝ *We have sprinkled you with our glory, our light. Now stay in the shadow.*

Why?

✝ *In order that they may see us, Nicole. We are moving from words to deeds.*

November

I promise myself that I will always write what Jesus says to me as soon as possible so as not to distort his words. I'm not very faithful, though, and I let myself be swallowed up by a thousand and one things to do. This evening I feel empty and without energy. It's been several days now that I have wanted to sit down and write what he told us, but there's just emptiness. I can't find the words; I can't even come up with a general outline. That makes me sad. Two times, while at prayer and then at Mass, I try to quiet myself down in order to hear him: nothing!

Finally, last night as I was rereading the Gospel for November 8, the Gospel according to St. Luke 17:7–10: "So you also, when you have done all that you were ordered to do, say, 'We are worthless slaves; we have done only what we ought to have done!'"

> Not worthless, Lord. That's not true. I am not worthless.
>
> ✝ *That is right. You are not worthless.*
>
> So!
>
> ✝ *Once again, Nicole, it is I who am acting.*
>
> Explain that again.

✝ *You have often said that your attempts to help or love or comfort someone seem empty and worthless.*

Yes, I have.

✝ *Yet you continue. What you did today in my name with Pierre—listening, loving in my name—perhaps that seemed to you to be both precious and worthless at the same time.*

That's true, Jesus.

✝ *The worth comes from me, Nicole. Beyond the apparent worthlessness of your attempts there is me, the worth that comes after the worthless. You act and I bring it to fruition.*

I understand, Jesus; I understand.

Then, a little later:

Jesus, if I thought that I had some worth, some utility, I would get in your way. Is that it?

✝ *Yes.*

"With all my strength, with all my soul, with all my heart," that's how I was taught to love you when I was a little girl, Jesus. I would like to add "with all my flimsiness." Do you understand what I am saying?

✝ *Yes. I am the one who holds and carries. It is too heavy for you alone, Nicole. You know that very well.*

I am worthless; you are worth. What a
wonderful combination!

✝ *Yes. We complement each other.*

Thank you, Jesus. So long. Come back anytime.

December

I've been asking Jesus to enlighten me about eternity for several days now.

Teach me about eternity, Jesus.

I am sure that if I weren't afraid of death, my faith would be a lot more convincing for other people. I know that he will answer me, but I keep on asking him as I am thinking about this. If I know the answer, Jesus won't have any reason to intervene. But I don't know it.

A few days later, when I am at Mass at the Carmel, Jesus comes to help me.

✝ *One cannot learn about eternity; one enters it.*

Explain that to me, Jesus.

In his homily, the priest speaks about the pope's book *Crossing the Threshold of Hope!*

✝ *One enters it, and you have already entered into my eternity.*

If you please, Jesus, could you explain that a little further. Give me a simple example.

✝ *For instance, you yourself often speak about moments of eternity, do you not?*

Yes, I do.

✝ *Those moments are prolonged. Do you
understand?*

Yes, a little. But Jesus, I love life. Look how
beautiful those circles are behind the stained
glass windows of the Carmel. Look at the light,
at Philippe alongside of me, at my friend
Martine, at the peace that envelops everyone
here and now.

We're at Mass, but I am sure Jesus understands and is
happy that I appreciate these down-to-earth and very
human details.

✝ *They will not be taken away from you.*

Explain that.

✝ *They, too, will be prolonged.*

So death is not the end of life, Jesus?

✝ *No.*

Please give me an example, a simple proof.

✝ *Nicole, why do you have such pleasant
thoughts about your departed Aunt Helen and
Uncle Paul? Why are you not sad when you
think of them?*

Because I know they are in your presence and
that they're all right.

✝ *There you have it, Nicole! . . .*

December 7

Pierre and I spent the morning with a group of monks, sharing our experience of the past ten years with the Companions and, first and foremost, praying with them.

As Philippe would say, "The wind was blowing."

Of course, Philippe meant the Holy Spirit. The Lord spoke personally to several of us. The three hours passed very quickly, and without knowing how I got there, I found myself at Mass in the crypt. I think those monks must have all swallowed a watch or an alarm clock because just a split second before it was time, they all knew that they had to be off somewhere else. When I am with them, I always have the impression I'm running behind. And I do run.

At Mass the lessons seem to be a résumé of everything we have shared, and I have the impression that Jesus is drawing us all together and that he is happy we spent that time together.

When the time comes to give praise, I thank him for these brothers.

During the Eucharist I cannot see the host because of the pillars. They're magnificent, but rather large.

I am standing erect and because I can't see Jesus, I say to him:

Here I am, Jesus, your servant.

Suddenly, Jesus is standing right there in front of me.

I am a little taken aback to experience him so close, so tall, and, above all, so alive. I ask him:

What are you doing here?

✝ *This is my eternity, Nicole. You standing here. Me standing here.*

Is this how we will meet?

✝ *Yes.*

Amen.

December 11

I was listening to a religious program on the radio this morning. An Orthodox priest was speaking about the tenderness of God for the outcast, the poor, the hopeless.

I suddenly got very angry. It's too easy to say, "God loves them." Yes, and then what?

> Jesus, one doesn't always see your tenderness.
> All you have to do is look at the poor people I
> know, at those who are in tears, the sick. . . .
> Where is your tenderness?

The response comes immediately, like a thunderclap.

> ✝ *You are my tenderness!*

December 12

It was one of those exhausting days at the Community. I had to listen, console, answer the telephone, check on the deliveries, make sure the kitchen and office were in order, and so on.

There was a procession of volunteers or Companions in and out of my office, each one with a problem, a question, or a complaint. I stagger into Mass.

I'll finally have a chance to rest and pray before I pick up Laurette this evening. She hasn't been feeling well.

> Jesus, I'm washed out.

> ✛ *I know.*

It really helps to be able to speak to him.

> Jesus, I don't have an ounce of tenderness left. I have the feeling that the next person to ask me to do something is going to get a brush-off.

> ✛ *Do not worry, Nicole. I will be there for you.*

OK, Jesus. It's your turn.

> I'm letting go. Go to it, Jesus. Do it!

December 14

Christmas shopping. How I love it. The treasurer, Jean, and I have decided that we will do something really special to thank a couple of volunteers who have done yeoman's work, and that's especially pleasing to me, because I get such pleasure from buying Christmas presents.

As I am leaving the store with my arms full of gifts, I bump into other shoppers who are all tangled up in their packages and wreaths.

This excess of material goods makes me feel ill. I love this time of year, but this consumer-oriented Christmas strikes me as rather pagan.

What about love, Jesus. What about love?

✣ *There are only acts of love, your acts of love.*

Later:

✣ *I am love.*

It's not over; that I know. We will continue this discussion later.

That evening at the Eucharist with Pierre:

Jesus, you seemed weary when you spoke to me this morning.

✝ *Yes. You want to be me, but that is beyond you.*

We will never be able to be like you. Is that it?

✝ *Yes. Do not organize love. Do not pretend to be me.*

That reassures me. When someone says that we have to love like Jesus, I always want to come back with "impossible." I don't dare—or rather, I didn't dare—say that. I know it's beyond our capabilities. No big deal.

I tell him all my thoughts. He listens and replies:

✝ *You will resemble me in my eternity.*

Thank you, Jesus.

December 18

Mary's visitation to Elizabeth. The Gospel of Luke 1:39–56.

Pierre comments on the gospel at Mass. Then he asks the little congregation to "share" this text. I listen, but I feel very distant from what the others are saying.

I'm a little unhappy about the way I am feeling, so I say to Jesus:

> It seems to me that this meeting between Mary and Elizabeth is an expression of the utmost simplicity. It also seems to me, Jesus, that this same kind of situation can occur in our lives today. We can suddenly start trembling because your realm bursts into our lives.

I let a little time pass.

At that instant I feel myself completely overwhelmed. It's a little like these two women on whom the Holy Spirit was poured out—a little like being seized by an eagle, but gently. There is no prey. There is nothing but the unfathomable that these two women accept with such disconcerting simplicity.

I am truly overwhelmed. I feel like I am foundering. If I hadn't held myself together I would have slipped off my chair. But I do hold myself together. I didn't want to stretch out on the ground and then have to explain to people that it was the presence of God that floored me and made me go limp. I want to stay seated. I do stay seated, but I weep.

This is what is going to come to pass some-where else, right, Jesus?

✝ *Yes. Not somewhere else, though, but with me.*

Deep down I know that these two women experienced this encounter on two levels: on the purely human level, just like all of us, and, more strongly, on the divine level, on the level of the Holy Spirit.

I am completely unsettled. I feel immersed in the divine presence and at the same time jolted by it.

It's difficult to hold it all together.

Jesus . . . Jesus . . .

Then I hear his sweet voice in response:

✝ *It is like me.*

Like you?

✝ *I lived on this earth as a man, Nicole, and at the same time I spoke with my Father. Do you understand?*

Yes, I think I do.

I am more and more perplexed.

Jesus, did you speak to your Father?

✝ *Yes. Did you think I could do otherwise?*

So that's why I am confused. I have a sense or a premonition—I'm not sure which—that it is this invisible bond between the Father and the Son that allowed Jesus to bear his cross to the very end. How he suffered!

✝ *Do the same, Nicole. Talk to me. As my*
Father and I did.

Everything is upside down.

It's overwhelming.

I have the feeling that I'm on the verge of madness.

January 8

When the host is elevated, I see the face of Christ in agony. His head is slightly turned toward heaven.

Jesus, you suffer. Are you in agony?

✝ *Yes.*

I do not even ask him what he wants to say to me. I remain immobile and present. That's all. Not only have I decided to let go, but I've also accepted it. Once again, it's simple and improbable. But "that's the way it is." He really is here. Period.

January 16

Just before the elevation of the host, I pray for the church that has been so shaken by the Vatican's removal of Bishop Gaillot from his diocese. I pray for Bernard, for the pope, for Pierre. The church is suffering so much, and then suddenly, without my even thinking about it, the image of Jesus in agony appears on the host.

Explain this to me, Jesus.

✝ *Nicole, I am here. I suffer with them, with those for whom you are praying. Tell them.*

That evening I sent a note to Bernard to tell him that Pierre and I remembered him at Mass and that I was sure that Jesus was with him.

Several days in Bangkok with a niece who is volunteering for two years with Enfants du Mékong (Children of the Mekong). Even though there are quite a few years between us, I sense that we understand each other. "The poor are our teachers": they keep us in touch with the essential and with the compassion of the heart of Jesus. It's a mysterious family.

A priest who is half Thai, half Chinese celebrates Mass. It is both spirited and simple, and a sense of unity prevails. This little flock of French people is happy to come together and share this meal.

I thank Jesus.

Are you coming?

Silence.

I would like it if you spoke to me. I've got two weeks and finally a little time for myself. Come and reveal yourself, if you like.

Silence.

Jesus, Jesus . . .

✝ *Let me do it. Let me do it.*

That makes me impatient.

January 23 and following

It sounds dumb, but it seems like I am running in place with respect to my relationship with Jesus. How difficult it is to let go even when you're not doing anything!

I let the time slip away. It's given to me by God, and he will quiet me down, teach me how to let go here and now.

We've had an insider's view of Bangkok this past week: lots of contacts with Thai people, Catholic communities, and the poor at the unthinkable garbage heaps of Nomkaem.

I love it.

Once again I am deeply saddened by the wealth of a few and the extreme poverty of the others, to say nothing of the scourge of prostitution.

Jesus . . . Jesus . . .

All I can do is repeat his name as I go from place to place, whether in the truck, or crouched down in front of an old blind woman, or looking at the charming smile of a stunning Thai girl in rags.

Your world, Jesus. That's your humanity . . . !

We're surrounded by huge, luxurious, empty buildings (probably a cover for money laundering) and by misery—and yet a misery that has a smile on its face!

> It is prayer that keeps this world going, Jesus. I know that, but it's not obvious, not to me anyway.

> ✝ *It is not you who keep the world going, Nicole. It is prayer. You just said that.*

> Explain it to me. Reassure me.

> ✝ *All those who pray enter into a relationship with me. It is this relationship that keeps the world going, but it is I who do it. I am the one who acts. Do you understand this?*

> But you do it in your way, and that's why it's still a mystery.

> ✝ *Yes.*

A few moments later:

> ✝ *Remember, Nicole, no agendas. Pray without an agenda.*

> Prayer of pure desire. Is that it?

> ✝ *Yes. At last you understand.*

Just a hint of irony or teasing. I'm not sure which.

The next day

In the mountainous region of the center of the country, we pass through villages that are very poor.

Families selling their babies in order to survive and other similar abominations.

> How can you permit such abominations, Lord?
> It's unbearable.

And a little later:

> And what about prayer, Jesus? Just what good is it in a case like this?

> ✝ *Your prayer, the prayer of all of you, keeps the world from cutting itself off from me, from us.*

Are you telling me that we prevent sinners from cutting themselves off from you?

✝ *Yes.*

You're going to have to explain that to me.

February 2

A fourteen-hour trip(!). I have time to continue the conversation. He gives me an explanation.

✝ *When you pray, you enter into a relationship with me.*

Yes, I know that.

✝ *We are two. You and me. Those who pray and us. We work together. Do you understand?*

No. I don't see us bringing about any change in the world. All I see is how messed up the world is. It seems like prayer hasn't changed anything.

Silence.

Jesus, explain it to me. Give me a clear-cut example so I can understand.

✝ *We bear sinners on our shoulders together, Nicole.*

I still don't understand.

✝ *Sinners are our children.*

They may be your children, but they're not mine. I didn't put them in the world.

✝ *They are our children, Nicole. We carry them together.*

February 4

Another fourteen-hour trip. We have plenty of time.

When you say "our sinners," Jesus, that's a little much for me, for us.

Silence.

And it's also too much to bear, way too much. Their sins are terribly heavy. Our sins are heavy, too.

✝ *No, you do not have to carry their sins. I carry them on my cross. I already told you that.*

So . . . what is it I carry with you?

✝ *You carry them in your love for me. Let go. It is I who love in you and with you. Now do you understand?*

No. What I mean is I more than understand; I sense it. This compassion I feel within me comes from outside me. I've experienced that already.

To be washed clean of all judgment. That has sometimes happened to me; it's true.

Did you love the adulterous woman, Jesus?

✝ *Yes.*

Doesn't sin disgust you? You know very well
that at times I'm nauseated by it.

✝ *No, it doesn't disgust me. It causes me pain.*

Monday, February 6

I am alone with Jesus. I'm back running the Community. The Companions are fine, but not the volunteers. Once again I have to straighten out their way of thinking and acting.

The day whizzes by and I take care of the problems one by one. I'm over the hump.

This evening in front of the host on the altar I thank him. It's a heartfelt thank-you.

Then I see the host slowly divide. One part is dark, the other light. It's not an optical illusion: I close my eyes, open them again, and see the same thing.

> Is it the world that is divided? Is it your heart
> that is wounded, Jesus?

No reply.

The image continues. In the open space between the two parts, Jesus is standing with his arms outstretched.

I don't say anything. I receive.

> You can explain this to me tomorrow, Jesus.

After a half hour I leave.

Tuesday, February 7

I go back to the chapel. Pierre isn't there and there is no one to adore Jesus. I don't want to leave him all alone.

The same image comes back. And Jesus is again in the open space.

Will you explain this to me?

✝ *There is nothing to explain, Nicole. Accept me. That is all.*

I accept you. When I say *you,* I mean the broken and wounded world, and Jesus, of course. How can I help but think about the church, which has been torn apart by the controversy surrounding Bishop Gaillot, and about all the suffering that this is causing the church's leaders?

I accept; that's all. I'm not going to get involved in a head trip. What I see ought to be enough for me. I make myself small and I let go.

Thursday, two days later

Pierre is the celebrant.

He elevates the host—a large one—and the darkened face of Jesus becomes quite clearly visible on it. I feel a deep peace. I had asked Jesus to confirm at his pleasure what I had seen on the previous days.

This is the confirmation.

> You want to say something to me, Jesus.
>
> ✝ *You remember about prayer. Our sinners.*
>
> Yes.
>
> ✝ *I carry the world. I am in the open space. I am there, living, in the gap.*

I think I understand. Right now the church is sorrowful and stricken, and Jesus is in its wound; he tells us so again.

As I am coming home from the Carmel, I can't keep from asking him:

> But still, Jesus, in what way does this make the world move forward?

I don't press. I don't want to put on airs, but in my own simple way I do what Mary did: I reflect on it. It seems to me that I still don't understand what Jesus is showing me, but I store it away, not in my intelligence, but in the depth of my heart. I tuck it away and wait. I do nothing more.

That's not my usual way, but it's reassuring and restful.

Is that how Mary meditated on the words of her son and her God? Maybe.

February 10

As I'm walking home, I stop by the Blessed Sacrament chapel of the parish of St. Thomas Aquinas. A little vigil light is burning. I pray to him, and as I do, a small, luminous cross takes shape. There are two bright little bars.

I accept; that's all.

Before I leave the oratory I check to see whether there might indeed be a little cross up front. But no, nothing but a little electric filament, I think.

That's fine.

Your cross. Your cross, Jesus.

We'll come back to this later.

February 12

The words of the pastor are refined and profound. I often thank Jesus for this man of God who serves him.

After a few minutes thinking about the cross, I say to him:

> You are the Comforter, Jesus, the Great
> Comforter.
>
> ☩ *Yes.*
>
> And the cross?
>
> ☩ *It is the source of life. It is the privileged
> place where I encounter my friends, Nicole.
> Do you understand?*

Yes, yes, I do understand. All of a sudden I know clearly and profoundly that all those who are suffering are at the same time given life and are intimately one with him. The cross of all those who suffer is engulfed by the victorious cross of Jesus.

It is a privileged place. It is the mysterious coming together of suffering and true joy.

> Does there have to be so much suffering in order
> to encounter you?

✝ *No, Nicole.*

I remember that powerful moment of suffering and joy when Monique passed away. We wept with Bernard, and at the same time, we experienced the overwhelming joy of knowing that she was with Jesus.

This must be something similar.

✝ *I did not die in vain. My cross is living—today.*

And when we place ours there, you are happy?

✝ *Yes, Nicole.*

Like you and your Father are when you are speaking?

✝ *Yes.*

Amen.

April 21

One more day and it will be a month since Philippe died. It was after a week of vacation in the Alps, where everything had been beautiful: the sun, the snow, our conversation, the peace the two of us shared when we got away from our obligations in Paris and Chartres.

It was the morning of our last day of vacation when he died of a massive, unforeseen heart attack in the hospital at Moutiers.

When I first got to know him at Chamonix, he was an alpine skier, tanned, bursting with health. It was a face even more tanned, more handsome, very much at peace that I took in my hands one last time before blessing him. He was still warm when I said an Our Father and a Hail Mary.

We were spared anguish, suffering, decline. Philippe left my life the way he entered it—softly, tenderly. His last words as they were preparing emergency treatment in his room were for me. The doctor expressed surprise at how calm I was (or very likely how out of it), and Philippe quipped, "She's a tough little trooper," and indeed my smile probably seemed to downplay the doctor's concern.

So, I've been struck by lightning and it's left me feeling like an amputee. It wasn't that I panicked. Even if I was anesthetized in a way by the blow, I was sure that Philippe was well off where he was, better than on the powdery slopes he liked so much or hiking in the mountains. A kind of leitmotif ran through the three days following his death, as though the words *All is accomplished* had invaded me.

Yet once more, my dear friend Martine came to my aid. She and her husband helped me with the formalities at the hospital in Moutiers and then got me back to Lyon and Paris. The way the children welcomed me, the warmth of my friends, the presence of Pierre, the Eucharist, the concern of the Companions, all told me that Jesus was with me.

On March 22 at the Basilica of Saint-Benoît-sur-Loire, I walked down the aisle on my father's arm just as I had at my wedding there, and we accompanied Philippe one last time. The church was bathed in light and filled with friends of Philippe, some of whom had come a great distance. His simplicity and especially his humility had brought together a diverse crowd. We sensed what linked us with each other over and above our differences. I won't repeat what has been written better by others about those hours and about the concelebrated Mass, but I can simply affirm my certainty that Philippe is happy and that Jesus continues to concern himself with me, with us.

The following days were difficult. We had a showdown in the Community. A young man suffering from withdrawal just blew up when we explained to him that he would have to go somewhere for a period of reflection before coming back. In this tight situation, I miss having Pierre at my side with his calm manner and especially his prayers. You have to face these things head-on, but this time it was just too violent for me. A big lubber who had come in off the road was the one who finally took over and restored order in the Community.

Too much. It was just too much. Without taking stock of my situation, I had pushed myself too far. On Monday, April 3, my whole body started trembling and my heart pounded uncontrollably. Finis for the Companions, my other activities, the telephone: I couldn't go on. For ten days I let myself be cared for and babied by friends. When the body cries "Enough!" you have to obey it. I obeyed and let go completely.

Now I feel like a spoiled child. For eight days I've been in Provence in a lovely house with a big family. What a gift! The delicate attention and the deep respect of each one and the shy but marvelously helpful tenderness of Mary (her name is Mary!), the mistress of the house, have brought me back to life much more quickly than expected. I've seen that woman every five minutes!

And so . . .

It's hard sometimes because some detail, something you're used to doing, clutches at your heart. Several times I've found myself wildly crying out for Philippe. Part of me has been cut away, yet I also feel peace and I am certain that Philippe is well where he is. This certainty is given to me.

Jesus hasn't abandoned me, far from it. He doesn't owe me anything, nor does God. Sometimes I howl with pain, but I'm not sunk in despair or melancholy. At least that's the way it is today. I don't know what will come tomorrow. I'm not planning anything. I'm just sure that Jesus will not abandon me. So I go on living.

When I went back to Saint-Benoît-sur-Loire a few days after the burial to visit the tomb of Philippe, I made sure to go to Mass. I was tired but happy to be in that place.

After the consecration I talked with Jesus:

> Why have you taken Philippe away from me, Jesus? Why?
>
> ✝ *I want you to experience other marvels.*

This makes me angry.

> But that's too much. Philippe was a marvel. You know that perfectly well.
>
> ✝ *I want you to experience other marvels, Nicole.*
>
> You can see, Jesus, that I am crazy enough to believe you. It's not because I'm exhausted: I believe you, but it's crazy. I won't even ask you for any proof.

My heart is at peace.

On leaving the crypt and walking along an aisle in the basilica, I was attracted by a bouquet of flowers. I glanced at it momentarily and read a phrase on a card in front of it: "Happy is she who has believed."

I pass by knowing that no commentary is necessary.

Several times when Pierre comes to the house to celebrate the Eucharist because I can't go out, I see on the host at the moment of consecration the whole interior grow dark.

We are in Holy Week.

> Is it difficult, Jesus? You mount your cross.
>
> ☩ *Yes.*
>
> And me, Jesus? What do you want me to do?
>
> ☩ *For you it is done, Nicole. Do not do any-thing. Your Calvary is finished, but I am still surrounded by a multitude as I go to my cross. Accompany them with your prayers.*
>
> Jesus, Jesus . . .

It seems to me that the hardest part has passed. He's right. It's only Wednesday (Tuesday?) of Holy Week, but for me Good Friday has passed.

A couple of times at Mass, Jesus has questioned me as would an older brother who's a little worried about me:

> ☩ *How is it going, Nicole?*
>
> It's going all right, Jesus.

And so we go on. Without Philippe's hand or his voice on the telephone asking me if "my pals" are getting along all right.

I don't know where I'm going, but I'm letting go.

Several times I see a group of men on the host when it is raised at the moment of consecration. It resembles the Last Supper. . . . I'm not sure about that.

What do you want to tell us, Jesus?

✝ *The world will be saved by a handful of people.*

Only a handful.

Why only a handful?

✝ *That is how my Father designed it.*

I promise myself to ask him other questions.

A few days later

I ask him:

> Why so few? That handful? What about the others? The immense crowd of others?

✝ *The others see this handful of people. They see us, my Father and me.*

Explain that again, Lord.

✝ *This handful is already eternity on this earth, one part of my eternity.*

You have chosen them?

✝ *Yes.*

June

The days are terribly hard for me. I am emotionally battered and left completely exhausted. June 5 was the birth of little Marie: my first grandchild. I'm happy of course, but not being able to share her with Philippe seems cruel. I miss Philippe more and more.

A new emotional plunge: Mother has been taken to the hospital for emergency treatment of a cardiac problem.

I feel completely exhausted, shot. I just can't manage to get on top of things. Too much is too much. I tell him:

> Jesus, look at me. I can't take it anymore.
>
> ✝ *I know, Nicole. I know.*
>
> Up until now I've been able to take it. What's going to happen to me?
>
> ✝ *You want to be Martha. Be Mary for now. Just be Mary.*

The days follow one another, slow, heavy. I accept it. I'm not rebelling, but it is hard! I can't focus my attention on anybody, hardly even on myself. I can't stay alone at the house, and it's a burden for Laurette to have to do everything.

I leave Chartres to stay awhile in Lyon. I allow myself to be coddled, and I repeat this promise to Jesus several times:

> I abandon myself to you, Jesus. I offer you these
> sad, slow hours.

I'm sure he's going to help me get out of this hole I seem to be stuck in. The medications help, of course, and I'm trying with all my strength—which admittedly isn't much—to accept the dependency and the low spirits I'm experiencing.

June 25

After the Mass, where I regained a bit of strength, I tell him again how difficult it is.

✝ *Just let go. Do not be afraid. You are my queen, my beloved.*

A sorry queen, Jesus!

✝ *Nicole, at this point you are making those around you stronger.*

My weakness makes them stronger?

✝ *Yes. You will see. You will notice it.*

Amen.

End of June

I can tell I'm a little better, but the days are still difficult. Some days the hours never end. Everything is slow, heavy, almost black.

You have to hold on and let go at the same time. I try, but now I have a better understanding of how people suffer when they are afflicted with depression. What a weight to carry!

July 1

I feel as if I'm on the mend. I'm slowly learning the patience and the humility of the body. My, but it's difficult!

I have lots of time to talk with Jesus, but without much drive I can only say these words:

> I abandon myself to you, but how difficult it is.

I try to let go.

Since I'm feeling a little better this evening, I talk to him as I'm going to bed:

> In some way it's because of you that I've taken a nosedive like this, Jesus.

As a matter of fact, it was earlier this evening that my strength failed me while I was trying to help a Companion who had gone off the track.

> You have taken Philippe from me. I accept that, but how empty I feel!

> ✝ *It is not because of me, but with me, Nicole.*

He adds:

✝ *I am with you, and you know that.*

Yes, I know it; I know it, but it's hard.

Sunday, July 3

I continue to regain my strength, and this morning before going to Mass I tell him again that I'm letting go.

> ✝ *I have not abandoned you. You are still my queen.*

I know, Jesus. I don't feel deserted, but I would like to recover the taste for living, the élan that I once had.

> ✝ *The hardest has passed, Nicole. We shall do marvels. I will give you marvels to perform.*

I believe you.

I don't know what they will be. I can't even get to the point of imagining what they might be. I'm living at the threshold of my resources for now, so it's day by day without any plans.

July 4, 5, 6 . . .

The days are still difficult. All at once I get tired and have to lie down. Yet I'm not doing anything but resting.

What a trial! I envy the people around me who don't seem to have any trouble running hither and yon. At moments Philippe is cruelly missing and his absence literally cuts me down. For better or for worse, I struggle to hang on to what I'm trying to do, to live for the present, but it's difficult.

July 9

I'm in tears from the beginning of Mass.

> What a cross, Jesus. What a void in my life,
> Jesus.

> ✝ *You make the others grow stronger.*

> Oh, Jesus, at what price. Look at me. Look at
> the state I'm in.

> ✝ *I know, Nicole. I know. And you, look at me.*
> *Look at my cross. It was much worse.*

Overwhelmed by that argument, for the moment I regain a
little peace. Jesus' cross, what an abomination! My soul
rests in quiet.

July 10

The weight seems lighter to carry and my head less cluttered with dark thoughts and fears.

> Jesus, I'm getting better, but I would like you
> to confirm what you promised me. I have faith,
> but you see how I would like your reassurance.

I open my New Testament.

Colossians 3:1–2: "So if you have been raised with Christ, seek the things that are above, where Christ is, seated at the right hand of God. Set your minds on things that are above, not on things that are on earth."

July 11

"Seek the things that are above"? Lord, explain this to me. I am on the earth, in the world. Explain this!

✝ *It is a question of lighting. Do not try to see the life I give you to live by your lighting. It is my lighting that counts. Our lighting.*

Explain that a little more.

✝ *There are moments when you are bathed in the light that comes from us. At other moments you divine a little of it.*

You know perfectly well, Jesus, that there are other moments when I don't divine a thing; it's just obscurity.

✝ *Yes, I know.*

So?

✝ *Just relax. We will watch over you.*

July 16

✝ *I will get you back on your feet, Nicole.*

I'm going to get back to standing on my own?

✝ *Yes, I will get you back on your feet.*

August 6

I pass part of the day alone. The children have gone off with their friends. It's always a little hard when they leave because when I'm left alone, I feel sick at heart. I stop at the cathedral awhile to pray to Mary. I break down in tears.

Mary, Mary, look at me.

I want very much to have her console me, and all the while people keep coming up to touch the statue. It seems like idolatry to me, but possibly I'm wrong. Who am I to know what goes on in their hearts?

Mary, I'm not going to touch the statue, but I talk to you and I know you hear me.

I let my tears flow. This won't be the last time.

Nicole, my Son is in your tears.

I know, Mary, but it's painful.

I continue to cry. I even believe this is good for me.

Mary, sometimes it's hard to follow your son. What does he want of me? What is he doing with me and with my tears?

He is teaching you eternity.

Oh, Mary, that word scares me now.

My head starts to spin.

> *No, do not be frightened. It is a momentary touch of eternity. You already have one foot in eternity.*

Mary, I don't like these abstract terms.

> *It is not an abstraction. My Son is taking you along with him. Do not be frightened.*

I'm not asking where Jesus wants to take me. I wouldn't get an answer. I'm in pain but in peace. It's true that he has me back on my feet. I'm doing much better even if my wound still bleeds.

> Thy will be done.

Each word is an expression of my absolute trust. My whole being accepts and consents. I go on. I will continue to walk with him and probably with the Companions, too.

The month of August

The days follow one another. I'm in the process of healing. I can tell even though I go on grieving.

I feel the warmth of my little notebook. That's where my treasure is, in my relationship with Jesus. I try to live the present to the maximum. During these months I've had the luck to have my little granddaughter, Marie, and her parents with me in a place where beauty and harmony reign. I've accepted it as a gift.

August 15

The cathedral is jam-packed.

I'm by myself next to a pillar and I shed tears: I miss Philippe. I'd like to bawl out loud, but I content myself with weeping silently. At the kiss of peace, a woman who works with *Secours Catholique* detaches herself from the crowd and comes behind the pillar to give me a hug.

We go to communion. God is here, his Son is in me, in us. I know he is alive. One must continue; we go on. I live day by day and receive the life that is given to me: the children, little Marie, shopping, tidying up the house . . .

I've decided to go back to the Companions. We'll start it up next Monday. I'm going to try. We'll see.

Monday, August 28

We welcomed the Companions. They're here, twenty of them, glad to be back. Bashfully, they let me know that they are pleased with my return. No flowery language, to be sure, but a bit of attention, a smile or look that tells me that they want to continue.

This evening in the chapel of the Companions, after the meeting, I thank Jesus for this day, for the energy that I have just about recovered, and for being inwardly at peace.

> Thank you, Jesus. Thank you. We'll continue
> with you, too.

Later:

> Your eternity, Jesus. I come back to that. Your
> eternity?

> ✝ *It is the present. Live the present, the moment*
> *that is given to you. Receive it from me.*

Sometimes it's rough, Jesus.

> ✝ *Yes, I know.*

The host is raised and this time I believe I see a cross, yet it's not the cross.

Jesus, those two lines that cross . . . Tell me.

I myself come up with the response:

It's like a gash. Is it my wound?

✝ *Yes, Nicole.*

What do you want to tell me?

✝ *I am with Philippe in that wound. Both of us are there.*

I try to accept these words that I find staggering. Both of them are here, in my suffering, fully alive.

A few seconds later:

Is this your eternity, too, Jesus?

✝ *Yes.*

September 1

After a peaceful day it seems to me that the Eucharist prolongs for me the gift of peace. The host is elevated. Jesus is here, fully alive. From the depths of my being I welcome this comforting presence.

We talk with each other.

> You know, Jesus, I've never been convinced that "everything is a grace," as Bernanos says in *The Diary of a Country Priest.* I'm just not there.

> ✝ *But you know that I am always here. That you can say.*

> Yes, that I can say.

September

Several times during the Eucharist Jesus tells me:

✝ *Be happy, Nicole. Be happy.*

I don't reject these words when I hear them, but to experience both peace and the cross at the same time leaves me a little disoriented.

Sometimes the elevation of the host sets my head spinning. Where is God taking me? This eternity, what an abyss it seems to me; but at the same time there's a certainty within me. Jesus is a living person and Philippe is with him.

Still September

It seems that the Lord still wants me to rejoice.

> That's hard, Jesus. I feel as if I'm not only
> Philippe's widow but also his orphan.

No answer. Just the same—I know he understands and I know he's here.

> I don't have anything but you, Jesus.

No answer.

> I follow you, Jesus; you know that. It's true that
> today I don't see anything on the host, but I
> know you are here.

> ✝ *It is I who am going to make you glad. Do*
> *you believe that, Nicole?*

I hesitate a little.

> The hardest part is past Jesus?

> ✝ *Yes, Nicole. I am going to bring you happi-*
> *ness, Nicole. Do you believe that?*

With my heart broken and my whole being maimed, I believe; I believe him. But I swear that I hesitate a little to put these words in writing. And yet . . . I'm crazy enough to believe him.

What's to follow? . . . Jesus, I trust you. We'll see.

September 29

With an aching heart I go to see Papa. After several days in intensive care he finally has a room. He is eighty-four. Recovery is slow and hard for him. His face is very thin, but the gentle warmth that I see in his eyes when he greets me is wonderfully moving. He can't say much, but the tenderness of his look speaks to me of Philippe. While Mother goes to Mass, I stay with him, hand in hand, saying not a word. Our deep, peaceful silence seems to me a moment of eternity. Under my breath I recite decades of the rosary. . . . Mother comes back. We have to leave. There's such love between the two of them, as if they were fastened together, that it feels as if I'm seeing them the day they first met.

On the train back to Chartres, I speak to Jesus:

> Jesus, I'm going to ask you for something. I'm not bargaining with you, but I want you to give Papa a little more time. I know, Jesus, he's eighty-four and this is the end of the road. I know. . . . Jesus, I have consented to Philippe's death and I do again today. You know that. For your kingdom, for the love that binds these two together, please give them a little more time. You can if you will, and I am your friend. I'm asking you for them. Do it, Jesus. Do it. Mother would not be able to live without him.

Beginning of October

There are three of us at exposition of the Blessed Sacrament. It's a moment of rest at the end of a day with the Community.

On the host I see figures pass by. Young people, old people . . . It's a little unsettling!

What do you want to tell me, Jesus?

I wait a bit . . .

✝ *I am not a tyrant, Nicole.*

A few seconds later:

✝ *I can adapt.*

Maybe he will explain a little more. I think he means that the faces I've seen on the host are him in his diversity. That would mean that we ought to welcome them all, receive them from him. The good as well as the bad, the sorrowful as well as the ones beaming with happiness.

I assist at the Eucharist every day. I don't see anything on the host. No matter! I know; I am certain that Jesus is really alive and here with us.

I have to get used to my solitude. This house in Chartres breathes Philippe. Everything in it reminds me of him, not only his watercolors, but all the little things he used to do tug at my heart. I'm not sunk in grief anymore, but it's rough.

October 15

The Gospel according to Luke. Of the ten lepers, only one came back to thank Jesus.

The other nine, Jesus? They were ungrateful?

✝ *Not necessarily.*

But one came back to you and that must make you happy.

✝ *Yes, Nicole. The relationship is what I desire. He deepened his relationship with me.*

A bit later:

✝ *I am alive. Do not be afraid to talk to me. I do not get in the way. I take up very little space.*

October

Here I am, back again at Moustiers-Sainte-Marie. In this peaceful sun-drenched place, surrounded by such beauty, I find Philippe's absence cruel. I imagine I see him walking across a field of lavender with his painter's kit, but it's a mirage.

I talk to Jesus:

> It looks to me as though you've heard my prayer. You have given some time to my father and mother.

Then I rather timidly add:

> I've already said thanks.

Later on as I am walking to the house, we continue our conversation:

> Jesus, you grant the requests that make your kingdom grow. Is that how it works?

> ✝ *Yes.*

> Can you give me peace for the sake of your kingdom? Peace of heart?

> ✝ *Yes, but you have that already.*

. . . ? . . . !

I burst into tears.

> Jesus, you can see I'm hurting. Here I am weeping again.

> ✝ *That's all right. Cry.*

> But I'm going to drown in my tears.

> ✝ *Yet once more, Nicole, you would like to be me.*

> No. What do you mean?

> ✝ *Weep, Nicole. It shows your humanity. It is your part.*

> And you, Jesus, what is your part? Is it peace?

> ✝ *Yes.*

He adds:

> ✝ *Do not reduce me to your suffering. I enfold you in my peace. You are my queen. The others will see it.*

October 31

On the host I see the peaceful face of a dead man. I don't
know how to interpret this; I don't understand it very well.
Too bad! . . . Jesus will manage to help me figure it out.

November 1

Elevation of the host. The center is dark. It has a narrow border that is lighter?

November 2

High to the right is the face of a man. This time he is very small. He is dead.

> Jesus, what does this mean for me? I don't understand a thing.

Later the Gospel according to John:

> You are the way, Jesus. Indeed, you are the way with me, with us.
>
> ✝ *Yes.*
>
> The way. Your way isn't in a little while, later, tomorrow. It's today?
>
> ✝ *Yes.*
>
> You walk with me; I walk with you. I already know a little bit of eternity. Is that right?
>
> ✝ *Yes.*
>
> And afterward?
>
> ✝ *We will continue.*

November 3

Always on the host I see the face of my father. I close my eyes, I open them again. It really is Papa, at peace.

> You are with him, Jesus, in his suffering on his hospital bed. You are with him, with us?
>
> ✝ *Yes.*

Monday, November 4

It's our wedding anniversary. I continue to be at peace; it is given to me.

November 6

Monday morning: Papa died at three o'clock this morning. It's seven o'clock now; someone has just come to tell me. I'm calm and I'm relieved for him. I found him completely spent when I visited him at the hospital last night, so before I left I made the sign of the cross on his forehead to entrust him to Jesus. Seeing his courage and his suffering, I knew there was nothing else to do. He smiled at me and made the gesture of gallantly kissing my hand as if I were a great lady. That was how we said our "adieu."

Wednesday, November 8

After a family Mass we go to the Rambouillet Cemetery, where, as Papa had requested, members of the Foreign Legion commit him to the earth. The moment is all the more moving because Thierry is there in his naval uniform to carry Papa's decorations. My fighter of a father is with Philippe, and now he really knows who I am. He sees me, and now he knows my struggles and my life with the Companions. He is the one who showed me the path to take.

November 8

I'm calm; sad but at peace. Several times I see Jesus on the host. The days are full and I feel healed. In fact, I really am healed.

> I have a request to make of you, Jesus.

> ✢ *Yes?*

> It's for one of my relatives, that she "de-center" herself completely. You are the only who can do that.

> ✢ *I will heed your request, Nicole. I will do it.*

I let a little time pass.

> Is it because of your kingdom that you are going to do it?

> ✢ *Yes.*

> Explain this to me. God knows everything, sees everything, knows in advance what we are going to ask for?

> ✢ *Yes.*

So everything is settled ahead of time. Then what purpose does my request serve? Your Father already knows what I'm about to ask for.

✝ *But we walk together, Nicole.*

If I don't ask you for something it won't happen?

✝ *It will happen differently.*

So why ask?

✝ *Because I am going to hear you. Without you, without your contribution, I cannot act. Have confidence; I will do it.*

You really need me, need us?

I go on thinking about this and I remind myself that God is truly the Entirely Other. I can't put myself in his place, but with Jesus I can actively join in his plan of love.

November

The Gospel according to Luke 17:6: "If you had faith the size of a mustard seed, you could say to this mulberry tree, 'Be uprooted and planted in the sea,' and it would obey you."

I let these words enter my soul. After the consecration I speak to Jesus.

> Jesus, I think I have faith—I am your friend—
> but I can't, we can't, make that tree budge.
> Explain this to me!

> ✝ *No, you yourself cannot, but your faith? Yes.*

> Explain that, too.

> ✝ *Your faith is our relationship. I am alive. This is a matter of my part and your part of a single composition. Do you understand?*

> Yes. What it comes down to is that you are going to transplant that tree.

> ✝ *Yes, Nicole.*

> And my part? To believe that you can do it; is that it?

> ✝ *Yes.*

November 15 and the following days

I can tell that I'm getting better and better. I'm healed in the sense that my body has recovered its balance. I've regained my élan, my taste for the present. I tell him so.

Jesus, I'm healed. I've regained my élan.

I thank him. A few minutes later he says to me:

✝ *I know. I will need it.*

My élan?

✝ *Yes, Nicole.*

Good.

No point in asking him what he wants it for. He wouldn't tell me. We continue on.

November 18

For the first time I see a sick man on the host. I prudently try not to read anything into it. Once more it may just be my imagination. I close my eyes and open them again. The face is still there, a sick man in pain.

When Pierre raises the host before giving us the body of Christ in communion, the image on the host is Jesus with his arms outstretched in greeting.

I don't understand. I say to him:

> Do you have something to tell me, Lord? I don't understand.

Silence.

November 19 and the following days

I don't see anything on the host. This doesn't in the least keep me from being in communion with him. I am sure of his presence. The days go on being sad. I especially miss Philippe at Mass and at night in my empty house. The presence of Papa stays with me. When I think of his death I feel an immense warmth and tenderness. There is nothing sad about it, for we said our *à Dieu,* our "to God," with such heartfelt love that I feel bathed in that tenderness. The words come back to me: "All is accomplished."

I have a sense of being accompanied and even sometimes unthinkingly speak to Philippe.

I even call out his name when I am alone. How I miss him!

November 24

I don't feel right. Philippe is not seated beside me. He won't be there when I get home in a little while. I speak to Jesus while I'm thinking of Philippe.

> Your eternity, Jesus. Your eternity?

No answer.

> Jesus, at the same time I feel that I'm being cared for very tenderly but that I'm also suffering from having part of myself cut away. Am I right?

He doesn't reply to me.

I listen to the gospel of the good thief. Some moments later:

> Jesus, your eternity. Is it today?

The word *eternity* makes my heart skip a beat.

> ✝ *Yes, Nicole. Today. Right now.*

This is already your eternity?

> ✝ *Yes. I have chosen you.*

But Jesus, it's harsh, your eternity. Today is harsh.

Just a touch of reproach in his reply:

> ✞ *Nicole, Nicole, I have always heard your prayers. What more do you want?*

But Jesus, I haven't asked you for just anything in these recent months. I've made requests "for your kingdom."

I reflect for a while and I say to him:

> I haven't asked you for just anything. As a matter of fact, you haven't answered all my requests.

> ✞ *You did not ask Philippe for just anything, did you?*

No, Jesus. Not just anything.

> ✞ *Or the children?*

That's right.

> ✞ *Do the same with me. It is in our relationship, as with Philippe or the children, that you ask things of me. Do you understand what I mean?*

Yes, I think so.

Jesus adds:

> ✞ *I will hear your prayers, Nicole. You will see.*

Every time, Jesus?

✝ *Nicole, I will hear you. Trust me!*

I am really torn in two directions. This rainy Sunday without the children is dismal, yet I'm also overwhelmed with joy. He can't lie to me: it's not my imagination. This joy, one more time, comes from somewhere else.

End of November,
beginning of December

The days are really full. I have to get ready for the annual board meeting of the Companions and not let myself get blown away in the whirlwind.

December 3

I think of Philippe and Papa.

> What more are you going to ask of me, Jesus?
> Sometimes I'm afraid. They are not with us any-
> more.

To be honest, I'm afraid there may be another death soon.

> ✝ *I am going to ask for your help.*

My help?

> ✝ *Yes, I am going to ask for your help.*

He adds:

> ✝ *Yes, I need you.*

During the following days, nothing is on the host except on Friday, December 8.

At the moment Pierre raises the host I see the face of Jesus as if he peered into my depths. Then on one part of the host is the face of a man. It's not Jesus. It's a man, maybe a religious, maybe a soldier, since his hair is cut very short, practically a shaved head.

> What do you wish to tell me, Jesus?

✝ *I place him in your heart, Nicole.*

I forgot to say that last night when I was meditating on the tiny bit of bread in my hand that is so fragile and *is* the body of Christ, I made this remark:

We eat you. You enter into us, into me.

Later:

It's absurd and it's overwhelming at the same time, Jesus.

✝ *I am not alone. The world, all those
I give you to live with, enter you with me.*

I haven't done anything more. Often during the day I think of that man placed in the depths of my heart. I don't know who he is. God knows him.

Nothing more for me to do, Jesus?

✝ *No.*

The end of December,
beginning of January

Sometimes I see the face of the Lord. Not always.

January 11

MASS AT THE CATHEDRAL

This time when the bishop raises the host, the face of a woman crying with pain appears. I don't know who it is. I pray for this unknown person, though not very well because I'm rather at a loss. Once again, let's see what happens.

Sunday evening I learn that someone in my family is in great pain. There's an estrangement or a deep misunderstanding for the moment. I was a bit shocked when they told me.

> Is she the one, Jesus? What do you want me to do?
>
> ✝ *Nothing.*
>
> Then why is her face on the host, and why are you giving me this confirmation of a sort?
>
> ✝ *I place her in your heart.*
>
> What do you want me to do?
>
> ✝ *Nothing.*

Who am I? Who am I that Jesus comes to place someone in my heart? Who am I?

No answer. I don't want to succumb to pride or to false modesty. I don't understand very well.

A few days later I pose the same question to him:

> What do you want me to do?
>
> ✝ *Nothing, Nicole.*
>
> Explain that to me a little.
>
> ✝ *She is in the depths of your heart. You think of her often during the day. That is your way of carrying her, but don't do anything.*

I try to listen and to let these words sink into me.

> What it comes down to is that I am to avoid doing anything so that you can do something?
>
> ✝ *Yes.*

He adds:

> ✝ *When the time comes you will be ready for her, for I will come to help you.*

I think I understand.

January 23

I see Jesus on the host. This comforts me and doesn't cause any worries.

January 24

On the host is a man. Then a woman. It's not Jesus. Why?

Jesus tells me:

> ✝ *Above all, do not do anything!*

OK. That annoys me a bit. I tell him so.

> OK. I'll pay attention, Jesus. I know that things
> will be cleared up later on. But just the same,
> tell me a little something.
>
> ✝ *Do not do anything.*
>
> It's your wish that I enter into your time, that I
> learn to be patient, that I speak when you wish
> and as you wish. Is that it?
>
> ✝ *Yes.*
>
> And that is also your eternity. Is that what you
> are leading me to discover?
>
> ✝ *Yes.*

It's as if in refraining from action I enter into his time, his
eternity, in some way.

The action will follow!

January 25

Driving to the Carmel of Frileuse to visit my friend Sister Claire, whom I haven't seen for a long time, I am on my way to another meeting with him as well. I know Jesus is going to respond to me. I know it. I'm sure of it. Why? I don't know why.

Here I am in this lovely chapel that is simple but strong. The sisters sing well. Their voices bring me close to their souls. This helps me.

The Scripture reading is about the conversion of St. Paul. What a turnaround! God's choices don't make sense. This zealous, respectable persecutor finds himself flat on the ground, stunned and blinded for the moment.

The free choice of God! What a mystery!

> You have chosen me, too, Jesus. What a curious choice, Jesus. It's incomprehensible.

I accept not understanding his choice. Nonetheless, I can't keep myself from saying to him:

> You promise Paul suffering for the glory of your name. Go easy on me, Jesus. I'm not Paul.

> ✝ *Nicole, Nicole . . .*

There's a tone of reproach in his voice.

A bit later:

> ✝ *I have never abandoned you. I will never abandon you. Do you believe me?*

Yes.

(It's an honest yes.)

> Can you explain to me now why you put these other persons in my heart?

> ✝ *Yes, I am going to do that.*

The Eucharist proceeds and I meditate on eternity.

> I trust that you intend to enlighten me in heaven.

> ✝ *Yes.*

> You know that I consent. It's all I have to give you. Nothing else. In the midst of tears, I consent.

> ✝ *Yes, I know. And now you consent to my timing. You agree to give me a free hand?*

> Yes, that's right.

I have firmly decided to say nothing, to listen but at the same time to carry on in silence.

> ✝ *Do not be anxious. I will not maim you. You will keep your spontaneity and your élan.*

> I understand, Jesus. I'm not afraid on that score.

Just before the priest raises the host I speak to Jesus like a little girl and ask him to show me his face.

> Show me your face. If you wish. In you I am
> rich, but I'm also a widow and an orphan. Show
> me your face. I agree to accept those you place
> in my heart. Show me your face.

And it's the cross, simply the cross. Two luminous beams across the host. My heart leaps for joy.

> ✝ *Do you understand now, Nicole?*

His tone is very tender. Jesus is tiny and it seems to me that he is happy.

> Yes.

This is dazzling. I tell him so.

> You give me these people (known or unknown,
> it doesn't make any difference) because at the
> heart of my being there is a cross. My cross,
> your cross. We are joined together.

> ✝ *Yes, Nicole, Nicole . . .*

Philippe, Papa, my solitude, my suffering allow Jesus to place these persons in me. It's not I that will act. I have nothing to do but consent. Nothing less than the secret, the secret of the kingdom: I consent!

February–March

I often see faces on the host. Some of them I don't know. I put them in my heart as Jesus requested. Nothing more. I'm intrigued by all this but still I don't seek to know why or who. I accept.

Mid-March

The anniversary of Philippe's death is hard to get through. How cruel it is! It's very hard on Laurette at this point, and my own heart aches more than usual.

Yet I have a kind of peace inside me. I have plenty of time to talk with Jesus since I've taken a few days off. When the pain doesn't swamp me I try to stay calm and listen to him. There is silence. The days go by and one morning I am able to say to Jesus in all truth—with my whole being, not just my head:

> Now I know what eternity is. It is Philippe, Philippe alive and waiting for me. Our love for each other has not come to an end. I know it; I feel it. There's Philippe and there's you, to be sure, but a face I know and love, a body and soul I love are waiting for me. Our love is not broken. See, I have finally gotten to the heart of the matter. When the time comes for me to die, I shall see Philippe. He will be my bridge. . . . But I have no desire to die right now!

This is the end of the little notebook. What does Jesus have in store for me? I don't know.